Special Acknowledgments

Thank you to my husband for all the years of encouraging me to step out and do what I thought was impossible. You are my biggest cheerleader and my love forever! Thank you for being you!

I want to thank Margie Fuller for helping me develop my thoughts after the long journey of ten years to birth this book. You are going to help countless others to achieve their dream, and you will see your dreams fulfilled in every area of your life!

I also want to give special thanks to Sarah Carver for carefully editing my thoughts. Your labor of love is not in vain, and I look forward to your first book being published!

TABLE OF CONTENTS

Foreword	3
Introduction - You are Called	6
Chapter 1 – Not Just a Pretty Face	11
Chapter 2 – Eyes Wide Shut	22
Chapter 3 – Intimidation Has No Place	42
Chapter 4 – Fruitless and Frustrated	53
Chapter 5 – What's Burning?	57
Chapter 6 – Top Models	69
Chapter 7 – Apples of Gold	75
Chapter 8 – Rest	83
Chapter 9 – Real Talk Uncut/Unedited	96

FOREWORD

The Lord challenged me to write on a subject that I desperately needed. I desperately needed this because it was something I was searching for but wasn't finding. I was looking for a pastor's wife to mentor me, someone to show me the dos and don'ts of my future ministry.

In this book, you will read about my bumps and bruises, the lessons that I have learned along the way and are still striving to master. I will share with you the pain that was administered to me by women in leadership. You may also identify with me in my quest to find my place in ministry and in learning how to work with my husband.

I want you to know that I do not write because I've arrived. I write because I haven't and know there are many women who are dealing with my past and current struggles. Let me assure you that although I have had a passion for over ten years to write this book, I have not perfected any of what I will cover. But I can say that I have grown in these areas through the years. I promise to keep it real! Being real is the prerequisite for change.

My heart is to be a helpmeet to my spouse and not a hindrance; however, my own issues and strongholds have prevented me from being as effective as I need to be. I am a work in progress, and my heart is pure in motive. I'm passionate about allowing the Father to help me be the best wife and leading lady that I can be. As you read, my prayer is that you will hear my heart that screams, "One thing I do.... I press!" (Philippians 3:13-14).

This book will help any woman in the ministry, but I mainly focus on the women who are

married to a ministry leader, and you are both working and serving together in ministry. This book will also be a great resource for those who are preparing for ministry. The Father may have already shown you that your future spouse will be a ministry leader. If you want to prepare yourself, then this book is for you.

As you delve into these pages, please examine your heart and stay before the Father to ask Him to send His fire to burn up all the junk that displeases Him. May He soften your heart, and may you begin to walk in freedom as you read these pages of love and admonition.

At the end of many of the chapters, you will find that my husband, who is also my pastor, was so kind to take the time to share his heartfelt perspective in regard to the topics and issues mentioned in the life of the leading lady.

INTRODUCTION

YOU ARE CALLED

So, your husband has heard the call to go into ministry. Hopefully you have heard the call as well. Unity is a must as you and your husband take steps of faith in ministry. The Lord commands a blessing where unity is present (Psalm 121). How hard it is to do ministry or anything in an atmosphere of division and strife! The first hurdle to overcome is to believe that if your husband is called, then so are you because you are one.

You may not have a pulpit ministry like your husband, but you are called to be a witness of Jesus Christ. Sharing the Gospel is not just for a select few. We are all commanded to "go into all the world and preach the Good News to everyone" (Mark 16:15, New Living Translation). So let's get that out of the way now. According to Matthew 22:14, we are told that many people are called but few are chosen. Really what that is saying is that many are called, but there are few who actually choose to follow and forsake all.

Many women don't want to take on the responsibility of ministry along with their husband because of what they have witnessed in the lives of others in ministry (looking from the laymen's perspective). It's an automatic turnoff when you see a dysfunctional ministry family and leader. Then there are those who were a part of a ministry where the pastor's wife didn't do anything in ministry and focused on raising the children. Witnessing this scenario causes those watching to give up on their dreams and visions of being used mightily by Holy Spirit.

Very few women walk in the anointing because of the pastors' wives they've been raised under. The hang-ups, hindrances, or negative examples and experiences we may have, or may have had, has caused to us not be who and what our husbands need in ministry; but we must deal with these things so that we can be effective. Our issues with moving forward will cause years of frustration for our husbands, who desperately want to answer the call of God and have their woman of God beside them. We must have the same focus and passion for the ministry that God has called our husbands to.

So, let's settle this in your mind right now! Don't read any further if you don't want to walk in one accord with your husband and in submission to your husband. The journey that God has called you to will be no fun if you are kicking and screaming the whole way. But if you have a yes in your spirit, and you want to be effective in ministry with your mighty man of God, then this book is for you!

If you have been in ministry for any length of time, there has been an opportunity for the enemy to bring hurt and pain in your life. The enemy wants you and me to become calloused and hard-hearted towards the congregation, the lost, and especially towards other women. We are nurturers, and it's harder for us to get over the past than our husbands. We tend to carry that wound and nurse it, or feed it, causing more pain and frustration to ourselves and to our spouse. Our husbands want to be "Mr. Fix-It" but will fail miserably until we make up in our minds that we will keep our hearts free from offense. Jesus said that offenses will come (Matthew 18:7).

I hope that what I will share in the pages to come will challenge us to receive freedom from the hang-ups and sin of disobedience, bitterness, insecurity, fear, intimidation, and manipulation. All of these can cause us to be ineffective in raising up other leading ladies. The questions we want to answer in this book are as follows:

How can I be an effective leading lady?

What kind of leading lady do I want to be?

What has prevented me from being a leading lady?

Have I been a stumbling block for my husband and the ladies of the church?

Have I hindered the flow of ministry because of fear?

Have I been ministering out of obligation or by being led by the Spirit of God?

Do I connect with the women in my church or hide behind a wall of separation for fear of being hurt again?

Am I an original leading lady or a copy of someone else?

From the Heart of My Pastor
(Pastor Raymond's Perspective)…

This has been years in the making but worth the journey. My wife and I have struggled to pull each other to a place of acceptance of the call of God for us into full time ministry. Often, we looked for

others to affirm our calling and mentor us in ministry but to no avail. We have had bump after bump and bruise after bruise, but we are still standing through it all! You can look to the following chapters to see a leading lady who has overcome and is willing to testify!

CHAPTER 1

NOT JUST A PRETTY FACE

You may have many misconceptions from past churches and ministries that have possibly clouded what a leading lady really is. First, let's look at what a leading lady is NOT! A leading lady is NOT called to be the one who shops the most and has the most expensive clothes, while wearing a mask to hide all of her imperfections. A leading lady is NOT called to be distant and untouchable by the women of the church. A leading lady is NOT called to be bossy and controlling of everything that goes on around her. A leading lady is NOT called to do everything at the church. That last statement alone will set many ladies free right there!

My definition of a leading lady is a woman who is called to be an example of submission to her husband/priest/pastor; she is a woman who leads women of the church or ministry. You may not be leading the "women's ministry," but nevertheless, you are who the women are watching as their example. When I say example, I'm reminded of the story of Queen Vashti in the book of Esther. She was the woman of influence in the Persian Empire. After her refusal to come when the king requested her presence, the king's advisors began to fear what could happen in the rest of the kingdom because of her decision. Likewise, our decisions and behaviors affect so many more than just ourselves.

If you have been called to ministry with your man of God, there is a place of responsibility and influence that comes with the job. Even if you have been in ministry for many years, I have experienced and found that women tend to lead out of a place of insecurity and intimidation, which are both rooted in fear. Ask yourself the following questions, and be honest with yourself: *Have I accepted my place of responsibility? Have I accepted the fact that everything I do will influence the women that are watching me?*

Let me tell you about myself. I was raised in a traditional Baptist church from the age of nine. My mother was and still is a faithful servant of God for as long as I can remember. In the traditional setting, she lived the best that she knew how to live. She kept my sister and me in church in spite of our absent father. Her faithfulness to use her talents in the house of God has made a huge impact on my life. She always said, "If anyone asks you to do something for Jesus, do it!"

I watched my mom be faithful to Christ and His church although our father didn't attend. He would come for our Christmas and Easter programs and maybe a Mother's Day. That never stopped Mom from going and making sure that we stayed faithfully connected. Looking back, I know that she would have done some things differently, but I praise God for my mom being resilient despite of her circumstances.

I loved to sing and participate in the church. Although I was in church and was active in many children and youth activities, I didn't seek God for myself. I didn't have a personal relationship with Christ. I had my rebellious years in college, but I would feel God tugging at my heart all the while.

After an abusive marriage and divorce, I found myself lost and disillusioned with life. I knew that God was real and that there had to be more than what I saw in my lifeless family church. I have no recollection of a pastor's wife making an impact on me. Although I saw pastor's wives, they never reached out to me and my family in a personal way.

It was the grace of God that allowed a wonderful man to come into my life at the right time. He wasn't saved, but then neither was I. One Sunday, he showed up in my church as a visitor, and that Sunday he went down front to give his heart to the Lord. (He gave his heart to the Lord that day, but we definitely weren't living a set apart life until a year later.) I saw him but didn't actually meet him that day.

A week later, I received a call at my job at the local phone company. It was him, but I didn't know it. Long story short, we talked that day for an hour on the phone before I found out that he was the one who came to my church! It was supernatural how the Lord brought us together. We were both hurting after our recent divorces. I shared with him my desire to grow closer to God.

After a six-month engagement and beautiful wedding, we were given orders by the military to report to a military installation in Northern New York. We felt God calling us deeper. As we were driving there, we discussed getting into a church with no drama. We desired to be in a place where the Word was preached and lived out. The Holy Spirit was definitely dealing with us. He was quickly taking the taste of alcohol and cigarettes out of my mouth. It took a little longer for Raymond to let go of these vices, but the Lord did it.

God was faithful, and He drew us by His Spirit to an anointed and loving fellowship of believers. It was there that I experienced a relationship with Jesus Christ, not religion as I had known it. My husband and I found out what a Christian family should be. Our lives were filled with learning and fellowshipping with our new family. It was during this time, we knew that God had a calling on our lives to move forward in ministry. Our stint in New York was our spiritual boot camp. We gladly served in almost every area possible!

Our pastor was a teacher in the secular world before becoming a pastor, and he believed in intensive teaching and training. He was a single pastor, but the ministry was effective because he had many strong couples that served in leadership positions to emulate a healthy ministry and marriage relationship. We learned from these couples, but unfortunately for me I didn't have a pastor's wife to learn and glean from at that time. I believe a pastor needs to have a wife, but in this case, I think it was a blessing to not be distracted by someone who would not be able to help me. I needed this time. God allowed us to connect strictly with our pastor as a father. We needed a fatherly relationship connection very badly. My husband lost his father when he was eighteen, and I didn't have a relationship with my dad at that time.

After four years of training in ministry (we like to call it our spiritual boot camp), my husband was given orders to go to Egypt on a hardship tour. This meant that my daughter and I couldn't go. During this time, I moved in with my father who lived in Marietta, Georgia. God led my husband and I to a beautiful, Spirit-filled, multicultural church before he deployed, and we were confident that this was a place that my daughter and I would continue to learn and grow while he was overseas.

While my husband was in Egypt, he began to walk in the calling on his life. After being there for just two short weeks, the leader of the Protestant service came to Raymond and told him that he was sent to Egypt to replace him. So, Raymond began preaching and leading the worship service. He began to grow by leaps and bounds.

We would have countless phone conversations about what God was doing there and all that I was learning at our church in the states. My church was truly a place of freedom that was exactly what I needed. I had begun to work on staff at the church, and I was exposed to countless opportunities for growth.

The women at my church were so inviting and encouraging. Although the pastor's wife wasn't active in leading weekly Bible studies or small groups, they had awesome women in leadership positions who were in no way intimidated. They were bold in the anointing and free to build other women. I like to call it "free2bfruitful", which was the name of the first women's ministry the Lord gave me before we were even in full time ministry.

It was during my time at this church that I saw how women can nurture and disciple women and how effective small group ministry is. I think back to a Tuesday morning Bible study that I had attended. The leader of the group was so in tune with Holy Spirit. In mid-sentence, Holy Spirit gave her a word of knowledge concerning the prophetic calling on my life. She began to speak the Word of the Lord right then, and the whole group prayed for me! Wow! I had never seen ministry like that! Her sensitivity to God was inspiring and caused me to seek God even the more.

I knew that Raymond and I would be in leadership one day, but I didn't know how all of this was going to happen. I longed for someone to mentor me, to train me for what was ahead. I knew that there were things that I needed to be taught to go to the next level. God did put some anointed women in my path during those years, and I learned valuable nuggets along the way. But I did not encounter anyone that was doing what I saw in the Spirit for my husband and me. We knew that we were called to ministering and serve full time together. I had a calling to preach, just like my husband did. We wanted to do everything together to keep the enemy out of the ministry. I had longed for a pastor's wife that could relate to our vision, to take me under their wing and say, "Baby, this is going to happen or look out for this or that when you get in that position or situation."

It was time for my husband to return home from Egypt after a year, and we were given orders to go to our next duty station. God led us to another Spirit-filled church, and we served faithfully for four years in many leadership roles. The pastor's wife at this church was an administrator, but she was not involved in ministering the Word, mentoring, or training the women of the church. I allowed feelings of rejection to mess with my mind. I couldn't understand why she didn't want to help me. I made the mistake of taking it personal, but it wasn't personal at all.

Through the encouragement of the youth pastor on staff, he basically told us we were going to go through a training program with him and his wife. This was the first step in heading toward getting licensed in our denomination. We are so thankful for that youth pastor being in tune with Holy Spirit! Our pastor had never encouraged us to go, but once we inquired about going, he gave us his full support.

At that time, I just couldn't understand how a woman that had walked with her husband in ministry for many years didn't have anything to offer us wives who were going through training. I had even asked her for her wisdom, and she said that she felt she had nothing to offer. Now I realize the severe deficit that most pastors' wives are living under. Ministry will knock the wind out of you, especially if you don't have a mentor; so, you must live in the fire of God and be led by the Spirit at all times. We will talk more about that later.

Upon completion of our training in 2006, it was not long after that when God opened a wonderful door of opportunity to serve full-time as associate pastor at a church about two hours away. We knew that stepping out would mean my husband and I doing it together. We are a team. If he jumps, I jump. It will always be a leap of faith. The Lord told us that it's either faith or finances. You can't have both. We left great jobs and a new home to follow the call of God on our lives. We served as associate pastors for two and a half years, then went into full time ministry as pastors in 2009. In addition to pastoring, we accepted an offer to lead the Black Ministries department for our denomination in our state. We also served as lead pastors of a second church in 2013 before receiving the call in 2018 for my husband to serve as the Administrative Bishop of New Jersey.

During the years of preparing to step into ministry, and now in a lead ministry position, God has given me a passion to encourage pastor's wives. Like I've stated, I was looking for someone to mentor and train me. Unfortunately, there aren't many pastors' wives that are whole enough to give anything to anyone. There is a level of stress that comes with ministry that some women can't break loose from long enough to see the women looking to them for guidance. There are women searching for answers on how to be a ministry leader's wife but not many leading ladies take time or care to teach. Why is that? Hopefully we will shed some light on that as you continue to read.

CHAPTER 2

EYES WIDE SHUT

When I first began writing this book almost ten years ago now, which has been a battle of building focus and discipline in my life, I spent some of my down time watching a popular reality tv show. My daughter and I would DVR it so we could just laugh and talk about what would happen. That particular season, one of the episodes had two female performers that sang songs that focused on the female power and how women are superior. Now I am all for women becoming all that they can be (like the Army), but there is a deception that has crept into our society but most alarmingly, in the church. The deception is that women don't need men, or they don't have to submit.

The moral decline of families in our nation prevents many women from having a healthy relationship with a father and/or a husband. Women have had to learn to be independent because of men not being in their place for various reasons. Because of this, their lack of submission creeps into the church.

Since the garden, the adversary has had a well-detailed plan to destroy the family and in turn destroy the church. The deception that Eve fell into was the feeling of not having enough or that God was holding out on her. She felt that she wasn't going to get all that was coming to her. That same deception is true today. Women feel that they need to look out for themselves, because they've been let down by life. This attitude in the church (and for the purpose of this book as a Leading Lady) is detrimental to the ministry. I had the same attitude when we stepped into ministry, although, I didn't realize it. I knew that I was gifted, called, and anointed to do many things in ministry. I just always felt that I needed a place and would risk falling into sin by allowing that attitude to get me out of my place of submission. I will talk more about that later.

We were created to have a covering. "But I want you to know that the head of every man is Christ, the head of woman is man, and the head of Christ is God" (II Corinthians 11:3, New King James Version). Our men are our covering. If you are single, your spiritual covering is your father; if you are married, your spiritual covering is your husband. I know this is elementary for those of us who have been in the faith for a while, but this is not popular preaching; so, there may be some that need a refresher course. Don't tune me out, keep reading to find out how this "I Am Woman" mentality is destructive in so many ways.

We have to start at the beginning in Genesis 3.

The serpent was the shrewdest of all the wild animals the lord God had made. One day he asked the woman, "Did God really say you must not eat the fruit from any of the trees in the garden?" "Of course we may eat fruit from the trees in the garden," the woman replied. "It's only the fruit from the tree in the middle of the garden that we are not allowed to eat. God said, "You must not eat it or even touch it; if you do, you will die." "You won't die!" the serpent replied to the woman. "God knows that your eyes will be opened as soon as you eat it, and you will be like God, knowing both good and evil." The woman was convinced. She saw that the tree was beautiful and its fruit looked delicious, and ***she wanted the wisdom it would give her*** (Genesis 3:1-6a, New Living Translation).

Notice that "she wanted" something and went after it without submitting her desire to her husband. She wanted more. Ladies, we must resist the temptation for always wanting more. We must learn to be content. Lack of fulfillment and contentment is an open door for the enemy to deceive us and ultimately remove us from our position as a Leading Lady.

Verse 6b says, "So she took some of the fruit and ate it. ***Then she gave some to her husband, who was with her, and he ate it, too***" (Genesis 3:6b, New Living Translation). Notice that she gave some to her husband, and he ate too. As women, we have so much influence that can cause our husbands to disobey God. Whatever we do will affect and infect our husbands and our ministries.

We must pray that our husbands will be bold enough to slap some things out of our hands (figuratively speaking). I thank God that my husband has learned to slap my phone out of my hand or anything else that could cause my downfall. He doesn't allow me to live in negativity. One day, he just got fed up with my little negative comments and told me, by Holy Spirit, to write Philippians 4:8 five hundred times! Ouch! That didn't feel good at all, but I couldn't get mad because I knew it was God trying to get this out of my life. That's not a short scripture either. But it was necessary for me because only the Word can break strongholds in our lives.

Let's continue on in the Word:

At that moment their eyes were opened, and they suddenly felt shame at their nakedness. So they sewed fig leaves together to cover themselves. When the cool evening breezes were blowing, the man and his wife heard the lord God walking about in the garden. So they hid from the lord God among the trees. Then the lord God called to the man, "Where are you?"

He replied, "I heard you walking in the garden, so I hid. I was afraid because I was naked." "Who told you that you were naked?" the Lord God asked. "Have you eaten from the tree whose fruit I commanded you not to eat?" The man replied, "It was the woman you gave me who gave me the fruit, and I ate it." Then the lord God asked the woman, "What have you done?" "The serpent deceived me," she replied. "That's why I ate it." Then the lord God said to the serpent, "Because you have done this, you are cursed more than all animals, domestic and wild. You will crawl on your belly, groveling in the dust as long as you live.

And I will cause hostility between you and the woman, and between your offspring and her offspring. He will strike your head, and you will strike his heel." Then he said to the woman, "I will sharpen the pain of your pregnancy, and in pain you will give birth. And you will desire to control your husband, but he will rule over you." And to the man he said, "***Since you listened to your wife*** and ate from the tree whose fruit I commanded you not to eat, the ground is cursed because of you. All your life you will struggle to scratch a living from it.

It will grow thorns and thistles for you, though you will eat of its grains. By the sweat of your brow will you have food to eat until you return to the ground from which you were made. For you were made from dust, and to dust you will return" (Genesis 3:7-19, New Living Translation).

I know that was a lot of reading, but it is a good reminder. What can we learn from the first leading lady, Eve? Well, since I've been in leadership with my husband, I have had to battle with getting involved in things that I did not submit to him. This was a problem before we went into ministry, but it became magnified when we started in full time ministry. It became magnified because of the higher level of influence that I had as a leader. The more out of order I was, the more I affected the church.

Part of the curse of the fall of man was that women would have a desire to rule or control their husbands (see Genesis 3:16). If you think about it, we have *more* of a desire to rule or control during our hormonal times. This carnal attitude must die to us. In the New Covenant, we are called to submit. It can be so easy to step outside of our husband's protection or covering by doing the little things that we don't think really matter.

Where was Adam when the serpent was deceiving Eve? Initially, when I pondered this, I thought that maybe Eve was manipulating Adam with her charm and sexy, hot body and that he was distracted. Then I wondered if maybe Eve had moved away from Adam for a little while and began doing things on her own. But the fall had not occurred yet. Weren't they made in the image and likeness of God? Didn't Adam fellowship with God on a regular basis? There was no knowledge of good and evil, and there was no law or sin yet. Satan was able to deceive Eve into thinking she didn't have to submit to her husband what was told to her by Satan.

My husband is greatly concerned when he sees women running outside of their spiritual covering by not submitting to their husband or their pastor. Women can tend to be gullible and easily deceived. Just as Christ is head of the church and sees everything, we must not be secretive or manipulative in our hearts and minds and stay close to our husbands.

The Word tells us in II Timothy 3:1-7 that there is an easy possibility that those (men and women) in the last days can come into households (churches) and make captives of ***gullible women.*** Think about it: *Why does it just say women? Why didn't the serpent go to Adam instead of Eve?* The answer is because women can be easily swayed by their emotions. The definition of gullible is to be easily deceived or duped; naïve, easily cheated or fooled. I know we don't want to believe that, but let me tell you firsthand, it's true.

I was raised to be very independent; however, I learned quickly that independence and being in leadership with my husband just doesn't work. It doesn't work in marriage, period! There were times that I would tell a congregation member something out of turn, without speaking with my husband about it first, and it caused severe problems. Even if I had a word from the Lord, it must be submitted to my husband, my covering, first. If I don't let him know about it first, he can't protect me from the enemy's backlash. If it is a word that needs to be shared, he will cover me.

Just reading that may make you uncomfortable, because you may have either been doing ministry longer than your husband or you just don't want to have to check with him on every detail. Let me remind you that the Word says to submit ourselves to our husbands in everything (according to Ephesians 5:24). Our husbands should be informed of all we do, even the shoes we want to buy or have already bought (and he doesn't know they are in your closet). Ouch, right?

Even if we are having a women's meeting, we need to make sure our husband knows what we are relaying to anyone under his covering.

These small foxes will destroy the vine. A little leaven leavens the whole lump. I submit what I will teach or my meeting agenda for his approval, along with the other leaders. If you and I don't submit, we can't expect the church to submit. Our spiritual leader will give an account to God concerning the church, not you or me.

> Obey your spiritual leaders and submit to them [continually recognizing their authority over you], for they are constantly keeping watch over your souls and guarding your spiritual welfare, as men who will have to render an account [of their trust]. [Do your part to] let them do this with gladness and not with sighing and groaning, for that would not be profitable to you [either] (Hebrews 13:17, Amplified).

If you are running outside of your husband's covering and not submitting everything to him, you are in error. There is safety in submitting all plans, agendas, and conversations beforehand. Your husband cannot cover you if you don't go to him first. I know this is hard. Pride and independence must go if are going to be a leading lady. We must submit to our husbands as unto the Lord. If you are not willing to submit, there will be problems in ministry down the road. Obedience is better than sacrifice.

> When swelling and pride come, then emptiness and shame come also, but with the humble (those who are lowly, who have been

pruned or chiseled by trial, and renounce self) are skillful and godly Wisdom and soundness (Proverbs 11:2, Amplified).

Every time I stepped out from my husband's covering and authority, it has been awful to say the least. I'm so thankful that I'm alive to talk and write about it! I bumped my head so you don't have to. Ministry will not flow right if we aren't submissive. I know that I'm spending a lot of time on this, but it's a huge problem, and we need to stay here until it's broken in our lives.

There are things that our husbands/pastors know that we don't, because he is the anointed one over the house of God. We can't think that we are equal in that responsibility. Those in the congregation call me "Pastor Lorna," but I know that my husband is the pastor. He wants me to carry my own authority in the position, but I will not answer for the church, he will. We must submit to his direction just like the rest of the congregation. He must have our respect.

Others watching us must know that we are respecting our husband's authority as well. Don't think that you will have this big women's ministry and not be in submission to your own authority. God will not be pleased. Don't buy into the lie that because you already have a big women's ministry that God is pleased either. Consider that God may be blessing your ministry in spite of your lack of submission and not because of you.

> It was thus that Sarah obeyed Abraham [following his guidance and acknowledging his headship over her by] calling him lord (master, leader, authority). And you are now her true daughters if you do right and let nothing terrify you [not giving way to hysterical fears or letting anxieties unnerve you] (I Peter 3:6, Amplified).

Ask yourself these questions: *What is my focus? What is it that I am seeking after? Do I feel fulfilled as a woman?*

> And when the woman saw that the tree was good for food, and that it was pleasant to the eyes, and a tree to be desired to make one wise, she took of the fruit thereof, and did eat, and gave also unto her husband with her; and he did eat (Genesis 3:6, KJV)

Eve wanted something she didn't have and went outside of her husband's covering to get it. She wanted wisdom, and it looked good to her. Eve was discontented with what she had, and she wanted more. Think about it – the conditions in the garden were perfect. They had a perfect 73 degrees to run around in their birthday suits and the perfect intimacy that she and Adam shared exploring one another. I'm sure she didn't have cellulite to be ashamed of or anything like that. They had all you can eat buffets of the freshest produce that cannot be compared with the top supermarkets.

I don't know how much better the conditions could have been. But it wasn't enough for Eve. She wanted what she felt she was missing although she was perfect. Did you catch that? Felt. Feelings. Emotions. The enemy was able to play on Eve's emotions. If the enemy can get us to be swayed by our emotions, we will lose our focus on what is important and true.

I have seen many women leave their husbands to do ministry alone and go off to chase their dream or lustful desire. The wife then barely or no longer goes to church but chases after anything and everything that involves her own interests and desires. I've also seen where the wife has gotten so used to ministry or hearing her spouse's voice that she no longer honors the gift within her husband. Her physical body is there, but her mind is elsewhere.

Discontentment in the leading lady leads her husband/pastor to a place of confusion. He will try endlessly to fix his wife's pain or emotional distress. This will lead to his demise, because he is distracted and will begin compromising his convictions to please his wife and soothe her flesh. This will then be reflected in mediocre ministry and lack of leadership. Next thing you know, another marriage and ministry is destroyed.

I can speak firsthand about being discontented. The definition of discontented is to not be content or satisfied; restlessly unhappy. Because of my various natural and spiritual gifts, I found myself wanting to be used. I actually needed validation because of areas in my past where I didn't feel validated. I began to find value in my job or should I say jobs. When my husband and I were first married, I was working. When we had to move to a new military duty station, I automatically figured I would get a job as soon as I could. I found many jobs, and my husband tried to encourage me that I didn't need to work. But I couldn't hear him over my own desires and needs. After many headaches and struggles that I caused, because I was so distracted with MY desires, my husband who was frustrated desperately asked me, "Why can't you just be okay with being my wife?" That stopped me in my tracks. *Why can't I be okay with just being his wife?* He needed me

100%, not scattered or doing my own thing. He needed to know that I was in his corner. At that time, I had absolutely no clue that God would call us into ministry. Dealing with this issue of discontentment was necessary for the steps that we would take later.

I see many leading ladies that are gifted to do many things. We can do many things well. I rarely meet a leading lady that isn't especially gifted in administration and leadership. These two qualities alone make us invaluable in any sphere of influence. But we must use our gifts in the right way, always submitted under our husband/pastor.

Share with your husband about what is going on in your mind and heart. If your husband isn't in tune with you emotionally and spiritually, begin to pray that God will cause your husband to be set ablaze so much that he will lay hands on you at home and keep you on fire and under the anointing. May he be so in tune that when he sees frustration and anxiety creeping in that he will take authority over it and command it to go. Allow him to speak into your life and then you must RECEIVE it. Pray that his ministry will be more powerful in the home than in the church. Side note: I believe it's the husband's issue of not taking authority in the home and being sensitive to the Spirit when the wife is allowing the enemy to deceive her. Many times, the husband/pastor won't confront his wife for fear of the aftermath. If we are humbled and love Jesus, our husband/pastor shouldn't have to fear our reactions.

Don't get me wrong, there are women who have been called to the marketplace. Absolutely! Please let me reiterate that this book is for the woman who has heard the call to serve with her husband, wants to learn about how to serve with a husband, or wants to encourage other women that are struggling to find their place in ministry. Regardless, we must find our contentment in the Lord alone. Contentment has to come from Jesus, because the people and things of this world will not fill that void. This issue must be settled before you and your husband embark on this journey. I can only share with you about what the Lord dealt with me about.

Let us keep looking at what the scriptures say about submission.

Wives, be subject (be submissive and adapt yourselves) to your own husbands as [a service] to the Lord. For the husband is head of the wife as Christ is the Head of the church, Himself the Savior of [His] body. As the church is subject to Christ, so let wives also be subject in everything to their husbands (Ephesians 5:22-24, Amplified).

And to Adam He said, Because you have listened and given heed to the voice of your wife and have eaten of the tree of which I commanded you, saying, You shall not eat of it, the ground is under a curse because of you; in sorrow and toil shall you eat [of the fruits] of it all the days of your life. Thorns also and thistles shall it bring forth for you, and you shall eat the plants of the field. In the sweat of your face shall you eat bread until you return to the ground, for out of it you were taken; for dust you are and to dust you shall return (Genesis 3:17-19, Amplified).

Notice God said, "Because you have listened and given heed to the voice of your wife...." What are we saying to our husbands? Are we speaking the Word of the Lord? Or are we like Eve, manipulating our spouse to do what we want? A discontented woman will manipulate to get what she wants. How do I know? I did it! By Adam listening to his wife, who was outside of the will of God by listening to the enemy, life became extremely difficult for him. God told Adam that the ground in which he had been formed out of would be where his struggle would begin. Life was supposed to have been easy for him, and they were to enjoy all that God had already prepared for them. Now they had to learn to make a way for themselves.

Your church or ministry will never run successfully if you are not speaking the word of the Lord to your spouse. We are called to be a "helpmeet." My definition of helpmeet is to help my spouse to meet his destiny. In Proverbs 31:11, it says that "the heart of her husband safely trusts her; so he will have no lack of gain." What are you feeding your husband? Are you causing your husband to gain or lose? Are you causing your husband to no longer trust God's provision because you are demanding so much? Are you so moved by your emotions that you are infecting your husband's leadership?

Eve stepped out from her covering, and the enemy was able to get them out of their position of prosperity. Don't allow the enemy to deceive you into thinking you know better than your husband does. You will then be operating in the same spirit that Lucifer was when he thought he knew better than God and could take His job. How foolish! The created thing could never take over the CREATOR of all things! Respect the man of God, the gift of God, and stay in your place of submission. If Eve was in the proper submission, she would have gone to her head and asked him if what the serpent was saying was correct. Don't make it difficult for your husband to lead you. If you won't follow his directions, how can he lead the church? Leading ladies are submissive and content with where God has called them.

I stumbled upon an example of a leading lady that walked in submission in Joshua 15. Caleb had given a challenge to anyone who conquered some giant inhabited territory, saying that he would reward that man by giving him one of his daughters named Achsah. Why would I call such a seemingly insignificant woman a leading lady of submission?

Caleb said, He who smites Kiriath-sepher and takes it, to him will I give Achsah my daughter as wife. And Othniel son of Kenaz, Caleb's brother, took it; and he gave him Achsah his daughter as wife. When Achsah came to Othniel, **she got his consent to ask her father for a field**. Then she returned to Caleb and when she lighted off her donkey, Caleb said, What do you wish? Achsah answered, Give me a present. Since you have set me in the [dry] Negeb, give me also springs of water. And he gave her the [sloping field with] upper and lower springs (Joshua 15:16-19, Amplified).

Once she had become Othniel's wife, she already realized her place was to go to her husband to ask him about her desire before requesting something from her father. Here is a side note and a good reminder: We are called to leave and cleave to our husband; therefore, no family member should take precedence over our husband, not even our children. Our husband's number one basic emotional need is respect. It is outright disrespect to go beyond our husband with anything that we need or that may concern us.

Okay, back to Achsah. She wanted to talk with her father about him giving them a wedding present. She saw that the place they would live was a dry place, and she wanted her new family to have plenty of water. She requested the area where there were springs of water. Living water! Another side note: A leading lady stays connected to the rivers of living water and will create a space for her family to be spiritually renewed and refreshed! Okay no more side notes, for now. It just amazed me that this new wife knew her place of submission. Father, help me daily to stay in submission.

Pastor Raymond's Perspective...

As with all relationships, we have to struggle with independence and overcoming our own beliefs, values, and morals to make them line up with the Word of God. My wife was taught to always have a way for your own provisions, so just to get her to have a joint checking account was a serious battle. We often had issues with her agreeing to do things without submitting them to me, and it led to a schedule conflict, which would turn out to look as if I was trying to control her. The truth was that God was trying to work out her independent nature. We all need to see that we should be interdependent.

Leading Ladies Prayer for Submission and Contentment:

Father, you know the lack of submission and prideful attitude that I have walked in and how this must have grieved You. Today I make a choice to fully submit my will, vision, dreams, agendas, and plans to my husband. I ask for Your grace to share with my husband all conversations and agendas with him beforehand, to not give the enemy any place in our marriage and ministry. I want to walk in unity with my spouse so that You can command a blessing on our ministry. Please forgive me for allowing my emotions to lead me. I want to be Spirit led and experience life and peace. Please forgive me for all the times I secretly covered my tracks or shared information that should have only been between my husband and me. Please forgive me for not staying under my husband's protection. Please forgive me for not being a good example of submission to my children and the other women of the ministry. Forgive me for allowing the culture of this world to distract me from my mission to minister to my husband. I am content in You! I declare that I am a woman that is submitted to my husband, so that we can fulfill our purpose and destiny and bring glory to You alone! In Jesus' name. Amen.

CHAPTER 3

INTIMIDATION HAS NO PLACE

Many women battle with being intimidated and feeling insecure in who they are. Fortunately, that isn't my area of weakness. My weakness is being prideful and overly confident, which is a huge issue! But I've encountered women in the past that were intimidated easily. Even though they have walked alongside their husbands in ministry for many years, they were intimidated by other women.

The definition of intimidation is to make timid; filled with fear. I have witnessed women who were called upon to speak a word or to minister in the altar, but I would see fear overtake them. When I asked a pastor's wife to mentor me, she told me, "I don't have anything to offer you." That baffled me! I knew that after twenty years of ministry that there had to be some wisdom that she could hand down to me. I believe that she couldn't give me what I needed because she felt inadequate. She compared herself to someone else instead of embracing what God had given to her.

Intimidation tends to creep in when you begin to compare yourself to others. Scripture tells us in II Corinthians 10:12 that comparing ourselves to others is to behave without understanding and is very unwise. Why is comparing yourself unwise? Because you can't become someone you weren't created to be. The woman you may be comparing yourself to has walked a completely different path than you and me. That woman grew up in another place, had a different family, different genes, different experiences, and so much more. Growing up in different places (living in diverse communities and cultures) made me who I am, and I am proud of that! You are uniquely and carefully handcrafted with tailor-made experiences that make you the wonderful YOU that you are. You have no need to be intimidated by anyone or anything.

Comparing your testimony, your husband, your voice, your body shape, or anything is unwise. It's not healthy thinking, especially when we should be fixing our thoughts on things that are true, honorable, right, pure, lovely, admirable, excellent, and worthy of praise. You are enough, because God made you enough!

When God called your spouse, He called you, too. You may not have heard Him tell you that you were supposed to preach, but you are still called. All Christians are called. The Lord says that we are "one flesh" as husband and wife. We must not fear or be timid when it comes to being used by God. God has given you a specific job to do.

Unfortunately, when we started out in ministry, I had a crazy thought that I was supposed to build "my ministry." You know, I thought we should be the stereotypical power-packed ministry couple where the wife starts preaching all over while the husband does his thing. That was my faulty thinking. To be honest, I had no clue about what to do when God called us to go into full-time ministry. I was going to do what I had seen, although I knew that what God had for us was different. Side note: Please dare to be different than what you see in the American church. Many are sleeping and don't even know it.

Ok back to talking about our calling. My first priority and ministry is to be a helpmeet for my husband, according to scripture. "Now the Lord God said, "It is not good (sufficient, satisfactory) that the man should be alone: I will make him a helper meet (suitable, adapted, complementary) for him" (Genesis 2:18, Amplified).

My definition of a help meet is "to help my husband meet his full potential." I am called to accentuate his ministry, and we function as a unit. There were many years that I was running in separate directions, because my focus was off. I was comparing myself to other leading ladies, which caused me to not look at what God called me to do.

Please don't misunderstand me; I think women should have ministries, but I personally don't feel that God has called me to do that. I don't believe He called my husband and me together to be focused on our own vision and leave the first institution unattended.

So, let us settle the issue of embracing the fact that you are called, because you are one with your husband. We must get rid of all fear and intimidation. "For God has not given us a spirit of fear, but of power and of love and of a sound mind" (II Timothy 1:7, New King James Version). The Amplified Bible version gives us little more insight into what fear is. "For God did not give us a spirit of timidity (of cowardice, of craven and cringing and fawning fear), but [He has given us a spirit] of power and of love and of calm and well-balanced mind and discipline and self-control" (II Timothy 1:7, Amplified).

We can do all things through Christ who strengthens us. Whatever makes our flesh uncomfortable is exactly what we need to face. We need to conquer that obstacle. If we have no interest to be "out front" in ministry, we should still be supporting and mentoring other ladies that do feel the call towards leading ministry with their spouses. If we don't, who will? We must be on the lookout for those who are hungry to move forward in leadership. Our job as leading ladies is to watch out for other leading ladies and be a help and support to them. A good leader equips other leaders to advance the Kingdom of God. Jesus said in Matthew 28:19 for us to go and make disciples. Reproducing ourselves in other leading ladies should be a major focus.

The women of our ministries are watching our every move. I have several women in my congregation that study me so close that they know what every expression on my face means. I watch other pastor's wives in the same way. When we go to ministry events, I look at the wife of the speaker to see if she is engaged in what her husband is saying. Why should others listen to the man of God if she doesn't? I make it a point to stay engaged in what my husband is saying no matter how many times I've heard him say it.

Confidence in who we are in Christ doesn't have to be prideful. It is confidence in Who Christ is that allows us to minister and be who we are supposed to be. I don't do everything right, and I am not the best speaker and singer that has ever graced the planet. One thing I do know is that I didn't call myself, but rather Christ chose me.

When I get discouraged and need to encourage myself, I begin to pray John 15:16 and say, "Thank you Lord that I did not choose You. You chose me, and You appointed me that I should go forth and bear fruit, fruit that should remain!" Therefore, I have something inside of me that He wants to use for His glory.

I don't have to be intimidated by anyone else, because I am unique in my gifting. God didn't create another Lorna or another you. You have what the women of your church and community need that no one else can give. The enemy's job is to keep you in that place of intimidation so no one will ever tap into the unique and precious treasure within you. If we are easily intimidated, those watching us will be, too.

A perfect example of being led by a woman who felt intimidated is the story of Sarah and Hagar, which is found in Genesis 21.

> One day Sarah saw the son that Hagar the Egyptian had borne to Abraham, poking fun at her son Isaac. She told Abraham, "Get rid of this slave woman and her son. No child of this slave is going to share inheritance with my son Isaac!" (Genesis 21:9-10, Message Bible).

Sarah saw something she didn't like when Ishmael began to poke fun at her son, Isaac. Sarah began to fear that Ishmael would take something away from her son, specifically his inheritance. Now the woman that helped her out when she was in distress was the very one she wanted to get rid of.

Unfortunately, the enemy can blind us so easily. Be careful not to hurt the woman who has helped you or is helping you carry the women's ministry or any ministry while you can't. Maybe you are the one who helped carry the ministry while the leading lady couldn't for whatever reason, and now she's causing you pain. She has forgotten your labor of love. You may have stayed later than everyone else to make her look good. You may have prayed and interceded for her situation. Now a flaw within her has caused her to fear that you will take something from her. Intimidation has come in. In whatever case it may be, when you have served faithfully with pure motives, the anointing will increase in your life. If those leading are intimidated by God using you, they will listen to the enemy's lies and try to shut you down.

Have you ever stopped to think about how Hagar must have felt? She was a servant. She didn't ask to be put in this mess. She followed her leader's orders, and now here she is on the outside and in a bad situation. Sarah had gotten in the flesh and walked away from the word that God had spoken. How many leaders have walked away from the word of God that was spoken to them and put others in a mess because of their disobedience?

My prayer is that as you read this book, you will make it your priority to seek God and not do this to the lady who is following you. A leading lady should be in touch with God and not put the ladies under her in a compromising situation, like Sarah did to Hagar. Sarah began to rationalize and reject the word of God by taking things into her own hands. In the end, a leading lady hurt the woman closest to her.

How can I prevent intimidation from coming in? I don't mean to sound super spiritual, but just spend quality time with God. You must set aside time daily to talk to and hear from Him. He will speak to you about your specific calling down to the little details of the day. He will keep you focused. Ask your husband what he needs you to do. Submit your heart to your husband, and trust God that He will give your spiritual head the wisdom and insight to guide you in the right direction.

It has been made clear to my husband and me that we are called to build leaders. This means that God will send leaders to us that are lying dormant, and we are supposed to dig out the leader in them and build them up. They will have special gifts and talents that I don't have, but I am not to get intimidated where others shine. You and I are called to allow others to use their gifts and shine! Don't tell them that you want God to use them, then shut them down when you think they are outshining you. Find out where that fear of not being the center of attention came into your life and ask God to burn that out with His holy fire. Remember, no one can take away what God has given to you.

Leading ladies are free to be fruitful. Leading ladies are free to pour themselves into others, so they will be better than you are and accomplish more than you have. Moses poured himself into Joshua, and Joshua took the people into their promised land. Elijah mentored Elisha, and Elisha performed more supernatural miracles than his predecessor.

Pastor Raymond's Perspective…

Because my wife had a desire to want to do the will of God, she sought after other women who she felt had achieved a position that she was called to be in. But time after time, she was left feeling so unfulfilled that she began to go to the extreme opposite. As with many of us who have seen a bad example, we often go to the other extreme to not follow that example, which results in another bad example. She wanted so much to have a mentor that she tried to become a mentor to every woman. She spent hours upon hours ministering on the phone and meeting upon meeting, regardless of our family needs. She felt that she needed to make sure no other woman felt what she was feeling.

Leading Ladies Prayer of Freedom from Intimidation:

Father, I come to You asking You to set me free from being intimidated by the women that You have sent into my life. I have allowed this fear to keep me from spending time with these anointed women that need me. I know that you have put deep treasures on the inside of me to share, and I will share them. Father, forgive me for thinking and believing that someone will steal my position or inheritance from me. You have sent help to me so many times, but I rejected it because I thought I wouldn't be needed or wanted anymore.

Please forgive me for not maximizing the potential in others. Teach me how to let go and allow others to shine! Teach me how to delegate responsibilities, so they can grow as leaders. I want to be a fruitful leading lady and not hoard all the great things You have taught me. I will sow into others and stay free from intimidation by Your power and grace. I command intimidation to go now! In Jesus' name. Amen.

CHAPTER 4

FRUITLESS AND FRUSTRATED

In the previous chapter, we looked at the touchy relationship between Sarah and Hagar. Why was the relationship so strained? Hagar was the servant and could produce; however, Sarah, the leading lady, was barren. Sarah was left feeling fruitless and frustrated. You and I don't want to lead from a place of barrenness. Leading from a place of barrenness will leave you with nothing to offer: no encouraging word and no power to deliver and speak into someone else's life.

Sarah had believed in the promise that God made to her for so long but ultimately became desperate to see change. Some strong areas of control and manipulation, which are rooted in fear, had manifested in Sarah's life. She was desperate to see fruit in her life. She placed the burden on Hagar to carry it out. Although Hagar may have been honored to carry the responsibility, it wasn't for her to carry. Has that ever happened to you? You've been given a task that wasn't for you to carry, and it became burdensome. Maybe you have a hard time saying no, and you've taken it on out of obligation. I've done that and still find myself doing it; this has caused great frustration to my husband, because I am not at peace and enjoying life as I scurry around to work on something that I didn't seek God for. Can I get a witness?

The enemy came into Sarah and Hagar's relationship, because Sarah, the leading lady, lost faith and her sight of purpose. She began to lean on her own understanding and stopped trusting God. Most desperate and unproductive people are led by their emotions.

The leading lady must be connected to God through devotional time (worship, prayer, and quiet time) to be full of faith and to prevent fruitlessness. Abiding in Christ, staying connected to the True Vine, will keep you fruitful in every season.

> "Yes, I am the vine; you are the branches. Those who remain in me, and I in them, **will produce much fruit.** For apart from me you can do nothing. Anyone who does not remain in me is thrown away like a useless branch and withers. Such branches are gathered into a pile to be burned. But if you remain in me and my words remain in you, you may ask for anything you want, and it will be granted! When you produce much fruit, you are my true disciples. This brings great glory to my Father (John 15:5-8, New Living Translation).

The leading lady must be careful to allow those following her to bear responsibility but not your responsibility. Unhealthy relationships will be the result of putting your load on the unequipped or the willing, innocent bystander. What happened between Sarah and Hagar? Hagar began to allow the relationship to go south by allowing her son to taunt Isaac. Sarah couldn't take it anymore, so she wanted to get rid of Hagar and the son that she manipulated to begin with. Asking someone to bear your responsibility to lead will never work out well. What is started in the flesh will always be flesh.

If you are the willing and innocent bystander that has taken on the leading lady's load, vision, or ministry, pray and ask God for grace to not become bitter. Pray for the leading lady in your life to embrace her position. The Lord may ask you to remain in place until your leading lady is healthy and can carry her own baby. He may ask you to just help her start carrying her own baby, or He may release you altogether. Be led by Holy Spirit, and make sure not to take on anything else that is not yours to carry. If the Lord reveals something, bathe it in prayer and submit it to your husband first before going to your leading lady. The Lord will direct you if you keep your heart and motives pure.

Remaining in place or staying in balance in ministry is key.

This leads me to the next area of focus, preventing distractions.

Leading Ladies Prayer for Fruitfulness:

Father, I yield to you and release everything to You. I place my trust in You to bring to pass every promise and vision for my life and our ministry. I pray that I will abide in you and that I will consistently bear good fruit in my life that those following can partake of. I realize that it's not by might, not by power, but by Your Spirit that anything will be accomplished. My lack of trusting has caused me to shift my responsibilities and resented others for being fruitful. Father, please forgive me! I receive Your grace to step into my place of fruitfulness! Thank you, Lord that I am free to be fruitful! In Jesus' name. Amen.

CHAPTER 5

WHAT'S BURNING?

Let me begin by first asking a question: What is your focus? What is supposed to be our primary focus? Shouldn't it be first to God, then our husbands, then children, right? I found myself in the most fulfilled position in my life. I felt effective and needed. I found validation by what I did. After all, I was created to use my gifts and callings for the Lord, I thought. I'm doing good things and people appreciate what I do. Wasn't it my job to make the church and my husband look good? Wasn't it my job to scurry around and take on projects that I could be proud of?

Many of the people of my church didn't know about all the things I was doing. Although a few would volunteer to help, I would subconsciously think that they were incapable of doing it as good as I could. Therefore, I would do it and couldn't hear my husband warn me to let go of these responsibilities that I had created. It wasn't until one night as we were returning out of town from a ministry engagement that my husband had to pull the truck over on the side of the road and confront the enemy that had deceived me.

You see the enemy couldn't persuade me to commit adultery or to pop pills or anything like that. But one thing that he could do was to get me distracted from my place of ministry. He could cause me to be scattered in my thoughts. It was like my mind was a racing locomotive. I focused on ministry so much that it was all I talked about with my husband and others. Tears well up in my eyes as I write this, because I'm so thankful to the Lord for showing me and delivering me from where I was headed. Even now, I see where the enemy has tried to creep in and get me scattered from my purpose of building pastors' wives.

There are good things that we can do and then there are God things. I would like to think of myself as a very capable woman that can do many things fairly well. I took pride in the fact that I could sing, administrate, be hospitable, preach, run a business, and be effective while doing it…Or so I thought. Satan deceived me into thinking that I could do it all.

There was a missing spot in me that was never fulfilled, because secretly I wanted my own piece of the pie. These were my thoughts: *My husband is being used mightily, but what about me? What about my dream? How I can be rich using my gifts and talents?* These are very selfish thoughts, aren't they? My motives were wrong, but I couldn't see it.

It was on a dark, country road when my husband was used of God to speak truth to my soul. This was my turning point! Side note: I'm so thankful for a man of God that will confront me when I'm in error! He is truly an accountability partner.

When we arrived home, I couldn't go to bed. I went to my prayer room and laid in the floor crying out to God into the wee hours of the morning, finally sleeping there. I then began seeking God's direction for freedom in the Word of God, and He led me straight to the story of Mary and Martha.

> Now while they were on their way, it occurred that Jesus entered a certain village, and a woman named Martha received and welcomed Him into her house. And she had a sister named Mary, who seated herself at the Lord's feet and was listening to His teaching. But Martha [overly occupied and too busy] was distracted with much serving; and she came up to Him and said, Lord, is it nothing to

You that my sister has left me to serve alone? Tell her then to help me [to lend a hand and do her part along with me]! But the Lord replied to her by saying, Martha, Martha, you are anxious and troubled about many things; There is need of only one or but a few things. Mary has chosen the good portion [that which is to her advantage], which shall not be taken away from her (Luke 10:38-42, Amplified).

Martha had the Master at her house, however, she was too busy to receive from Him. She was focused on all the things that she had going on. This included: ministry events, upcoming dates, family issues, and all of the other irons that she had in the fire. If I can warn you of anything, refuse to allow distractions to stay in your mind. They will come but take those thoughts captive.

Let me give you the definition of distracted. Distracted means to have extreme confusion of the mind; to have your attention diverted; lack of focus; to draw away or pull apart from.[1] The enemy's job is to attack the mind. His desire is to see us distracted from our priority, which is our relationship with God and our spouse.

If our focus has been on our children, I hate to upset the applecart, but we are out of order. If our focus is on our relationship with God and then our spouse, the children will always fall right into place. We create a desire for marriage in our children when we show them the proper order and respect for our spouses. Our husbands must know that they are more important than anything else on the planet!

Let's get back to the word "distracted." Women are notorious for being distracted. I can walk into my closet to get a blanket, begin to think about the weekend, and then I'm trying to find something to wear for the event. Next, I'm making a pile of things that need to go to the cleaners; before I know it, thirty precious minutes have passed, and all I intended to do was get a blanket! Can you relate?

What about getting on the computer? I can sit down and have one thing on my mind to do; before I know it, a pop up or two or a message from Facebook comes up. You know how that rabbit trail begins and ends! I have wasted time because of distractions! I'm so tired of losing precious time in my life to distractions.

Can I tell you this? Ministry doesn't slow down. It's mandatory that we stay in the flow of the living water to remain fresh and balanced. Currently, I serve as an associate pastor, worship pastor, lead the women's ministry, assist my husband in a state ministry, teach a Life

Group class, serve on a state-elected board, serve as a director for the Chamber of Commerce, serve on a regional ministry board, serve in a parachurch organization, and any other thing that my husband may need me to do.

When I first started writing this book over ten years ago, I had only a few things on my plate. I can't explain how it all gets done. I do know that I have to focus and refuse distractions by prioritizing my time with Jesus. When I do this, He gives me wisdom and supernatural downloads on how and when to do what I need to do.

Leading ladies must be focused. So I'm going to jump right into a serious lack in the marital, ministry relationship. In ministry, our husbands need to know that we are focused on their sexual and emotional needs. Unfortunately, many pastors and leaders have fallen prey to the enemy through sexual sin, because their wives were distracted with something else.

I would climb into the bed so tired from my day that I was mentally checked out when being physically intimate with my husband. Did that make him feel special? Absolutely not. He asked me, "When was the last time you prepared a candlelight dinner?" or "When was the last time you scheduled a special time just for us?" When he asked me that, my first response was to get offended and ask him the same question. But when my eyes were opened, it was true. It had been a long while since I had made him a high priority in my mind.

We have to spend time seeking God on how to bless our husbands then be obedient to what He says to do. Holy Spirit will give you very good directions on how to bless and serve your husband.

The enemy's job is to keep us distracted from our God-given priorities. Don't allow him to keep you distracted from your destiny, your desires, and your dreams. To be distracted is the opposite of being balanced. Balance is mental steadiness or emotional stability. How many women do you know that are emotionally unstable? I am a witness to that myself! Being a balanced woman includes maintaining calm behavior and judgment. Lord, help me!

Martha, in our text, was distracted or divided into parts. Matthew 6:25 says, "Therefore I tell you, stop being perpetually uneasy (anxious and worried) about your life, what you shall eat or what you shall drink;

or about your body, what you shall put on. Is not life greater [in quality] than food, and the body [far above and more excellent] than clothing?" The word *worried* in the Greek language is the same word for distracted or preoccupied with things causing stress, anxiety, and pressure culminating in disease or physical sickness. Why is there so much sickness and disease in the body of Christ? Maybe because we are so distracted and preoccupied with everything else but Christ.

As I continued studying about being distracted, the Lord gave me this revelation through the Word:

> I know your industry and activities, laborious toil and trouble, and your patient endurance, and how you cannot tolerate wicked [men] and have tested and critically appraised those who call [themselves] apostles (special messengers of Christ) and yet are not, and have found them to be impostors and liars. I know you are enduring patiently and are bearing up for My name's sake, and you have not fainted or become exhausted or grown weary.4 But I have this [one charge to make] against you: that you have left (abandoned) the love that you had at first [you have deserted Me, your first love]. Remember then from what heights you have fallen. Repent (change the inner man to meet God's will) and do the works you did previously [when first you knew the Lord], or else I will visit you and remove your lampstand from its place, unless you change your mind and repent (Revelation 2:2-5, Amplified).

The church of Ephesus was known for its hard work and patient endurance, but they also had a problem with distraction. The word *left* in verse 4 is the same Greek work *aphiemi,* which means distracted or drawn apart. Therefore, the church of Ephesus had become distracted from who they should have been focusing on – Christ. They were doing good things that Christ gave them commendation for, but we can do great things and leave the most important element out of it. My husband always says, "We can do good things, but is it a God thing?"

Jesus said in verse 5 that they needed to repent, or they will be removed from their place. Out of all of the seven churches, this was the only church that Jesus said this to. When I think of a lampstand, I think of a candle. When a candle has been removed, the flame has been extinguished, leaving the smell of smoke. What is burning now? If God removes you or me because of distraction, we will experience the smell of smoke in hell. We don't want that.

Martha could have been distracted and worried about burning the food that was cooking. The very thing that distracted Martha could have been the very thing to destroy her. What is distracting you and me? Did you realize that distractions could cause us to be removed from our current position?

It was a humbling moment when the Lord showed me that I had been prideful in my distractions, making excuses for my prideful endeavors. I thought it was my job to take on projects and responsibilities to make my husband and our ministry look good. Besides, I thought no one else could do what I do. But after the Lord showed me about the church of Ephesus being removed if they didn't repent from their distractions, I realized that I, too, can be removed from my place. He could raise up another woman to help my husband reach his destiny. Needless to say, that was enough to get me back on the right track.

I don't need to head up another program or ministry. As a matter of fact, I don't need to do anything just because the previous leading lady may have done it. My job is to be a helpmeet to my husband – to help my husband meet his destiny. If he tells me that he needs me to do it, then I will. No longer will I take on responsibilities for myself.

I recently heard a great acronym for BUSY – Being Under Satan's Yoke. If you are just too busy, then the enemy has distracted you from what really matters. A great man of God once said, "If Satan can't slow you down, then he will speed you up!" I had gotten so busy that I couldn't slow my mind down. So please, woman of God, don't allow the enemy to distract you. Stay balanced and focused. Being distracted will cause you to be removed from your place of destiny, and He will raise someone else up to do what you should be doing.

> Looking away [from all that will distract] to Jesus, Who is the Leader and the Source of our faith [giving the first incentive for our belief] and is also its Finisher [bringing it to maturity and perfection]. He, for the joy [of obtaining the prize] that was set before Him, endured the cross, despising and ignoring the shame, and is now seated at the right hand of the throne of God (Hebrews 12:2, Amplified).

I love what Hebrews says about distraction. As long as we keep our eyes focused on Christ, distractions will no longer delay the great things that God wants to do in and through us.

Leading Ladies Prayer for Focus and Balance:

Father, I worship You and You alone. May You be my supreme focus, and may I prioritize the tasks and responsibilities that You give. Lord, help me to make sure that my spouse knows that he is my human priority on earth. May everyone and everything else fall in the proper place in my life. Father, I repent of being distracted and for allowing distractions to come in. Lord, I want to acknowledge You in all of my ways and forever be willing to listen to You no matter what may be burning on the stove. Please help me to be a good example to the women who are watching me, as I put You first and honor and respect my husband by giving him my undivided attention. I love you, Lord. In Jesus' name. Amen.

[1]Definition of word – distraction - Dictionary.com

CHAPTER 6

TOP MODELS

For years I have longed to have a role model (leading lady) in my life, someone to inspire me, challenge me, and someone that could speak purpose and destiny into my life. Many other women are looking for that someone, too. If you are a leading lady, there are women watching you, and they are secretly hoping that you will be an example to them. They are in need of someone to answer the questions that they haven't quite formulated and how to even relay those questions. The magnitude of the God-given vision may be so big that they don't even know what to ask. They just simply need your wisdom, experience, and encouragement.

As we previously discussed, women tend to be in competition with one another or compare themselves with other women. Older women are intimidated by a younger woman. Younger women are intimidated by a wise, anointed woman. It really shouldn't be that way. Why can't we begin to celebrate and encourage one another?

A picture of the older encouraging the younger is Mary and Elizabeth, found in Luke 1:26-56. Elizabeth is a top model in my book! Mary, a young and inexperienced girl, has just had a bomb dropped on her that she will carry the Anointed One in her womb! She is going to carry the Messiah, the Redeemer of mankind! Our mission (waiting on the next speaking engagement or planning a women's conference) pales in comparison to hers, doesn't it? She has had a visit from one of the archangels! No wonder she just pondered this in her heart! It was too big to even repeat!

The angel, Gabriel, told Mary that her relative, Elizabeth, was pregnant. Mary had to know that only God could have blessed her relative, who was up in age, to get pregnant (and at this point was six months along). It's powerful to me that God will connect you with someone else in a supernatural situation to confirm to you that you are on the right track. Supernatural! Mary probably would have doubted everything if she didn't have some earthly proof that her old and barren relative was pregnant. She must have thought, *If she's pregnant I know that God can do anything!*

Mary must have needed to get confirmation. I mean, wouldn't you? Just a few days later she went to visit Elizabeth. When she walked in the room, the baby leaped in Elizabeth's womb, and Elizabeth was filled with Holy Spirit (Luke 1:41). A leading lady will connect with another leading lady and supernatural things will happen. God will give you a leading lady. He will put that leading lady, who you have desperately desired for, in your path.

There was no intimidation in Mary and Elizabeth's relationship, only connection in the spirit. Elizabeth began to encourage Mary by speaking life into her spirit (Luke 1:42). Elizabeth confirmed what God was doing in Mary before Mary had even opened her mouth. We need a leading lady who can pick up on what's going on inside of you even before you open your mouth. You and I need someone that is in tune with Holy Spirit!

Elizabeth could speak life, because the Lord had filled her with life! Don't get around women that are always fearful of what you may take from them; on the other hand, don't be fearful or envious of what others have. What God has for you is for you! I know I've said this before, but

I need to say it again: Please don't compare yourself against any other woman. You don't know what others have had to walk through to have what they have now.

Why do I call Mary and Elizabeth model leading ladies? It's because they weren't afraid to share with one another. Each was free to carry her own ministry yet encourage the other. One was called to carry her ministry/baby in a later season in her life, while the other was having to carry hers in her young and inexperienced season. God was doing something in them and through them that others definitely couldn't understand or comprehend. They needed each other!

In my life, I find so much refreshment and encouragement by getting together with another leading lady. We talk about our challenges and victories, usually over a cup of coffee. Oh, how I love coffee! I find out that what I'm going through isn't foreign, and that I'm going to get through this. Most of the time, my leading lady friend is experiencing something that I've been through. I'm able to listen and help, and it works vice versa.

The enemy likes to keep us from feeling like we can't talk to anyone or that we don't need to bother anyone. If the enemy can get us on an island to ourselves and lonely, he can destroy us. But if we get together with another leading lady, we come away refreshed and much stronger.

Leading ladies must be secure in their station in life. If God has called you to a big church, amen! If God had called you to have a Bible study in your living room, amen! There are no big I's or little u's in the body of Christ. There are women that God has sent in your path who are carrying a supernatural baby, and they need a leading lady that can relate to carrying something bigger than life. You can't explain what you feel and what you know – you just know! You need someone that can connect with you on that level, and it has nothing to do with age or knowledge. It's supernatural!

Pastor Raymond's Perspective...

As the Lord began to balance my wife's self-effort to try and feel validated within herself, she began to focus on the main thing of importance, being a helpmeet. Yes, she had her struggles. Yes, she met opposition. But victory was achieved once she got to the position that God ordained her to have: first as wife, second as mom, and third as leading lady. This order ultimately led to being a leading lady in word and in deed. She has become a great leading lady by first putting everything in perspective. Now I have no problem with

her leading women's ministry, because I know she's not doing it to feel fulfilled. She's doing it to fulfill her calling. She's called, chosen, and comfortable knowing she is my wife. I believe that every wife who is called to lead should launch from a position of rest and security and not from a place of starting and then trying to figure everything out.

CHAPTER 7

APPLES OF GOLD

There are three scriptures that I would like to reference for this chapter. "Timely advice is lovely, like golden apples in a silver basket" (Proverbs 25:11, New Living Translation). "A word fitly spoken is like apples of gold in settings of silver" (Proverbs 25:11, New King James Version). "She opens her mouth with wisdom, and on her tongue is the law of kindness" (Proverbs 31:26, New King James Version).

Our influence to our husbands lives is tantamount to God's voice. Our husbands trust that when we speak, we are speaking truth and with wisdom. Most wise husbands understand that women have a special insight that only God can give. My husband has said that if he comes to a situation when I'm not around, that God's voice sounds like my voice in his head. That's powerful that God would use my voice to speak wisdom and insight in his spirit! So, 3I hope that you are getting the picture that what we say, how we say it, and when we say things makes a huge impact on our spouses.

In ministry, our husbands go through seasons of insecurity and struggle to know if they are
leading in the right direction. Many times, they are secretly desiring for confirmation, and who else would they desire confirmation from? They desire this from those closest to them, more specifically their wives. Your husband is hoping that you have heard from the Lord and are spending time with the Lord. I must confess that I don't spend as much time with the Lord as I would like to, but my desire is to be in tune and not a distraction for my husband. I want to be a help and not a hindrance to our marriage and ministry. I'm so glad that the Father looks at the heart of man and not the outward appearance!

You see, we have a choice to make. I'll show you some biblical examples of being a help or a hindrance to your husband's ministry. First, we will take a look at Zeresh's wife in Esther chapter five. I'm sure you are familiar with the book of Esther, because she is a great example of a leading lady. She made a huge sacrifice for her people and took great risks. She fasted and set herself apart for a selfless purpose. Side note: Are we willing to go the extra mile? Sadly, my intentions are good, but I don't follow through with my inner man's desire to go deeper on behalf of someone else's freedom.

Anyway, back to Esther. Haman had an evil intention to destroy Esther's people, and unfortunately, he had a wife that led him in the wrong direction. Let's read about this in Esther Chapter 5.

> Now it happened on the third day that Esther put on her royal robes and stood in the inner court of the king's palace, across from the king's house, while the king sat on his royal throne in the royal house, facing the entrance of the house. So it was, when the king saw Queen Esther standing in the court, that she found favor in his sight, and the king held out to Esther the golden scepter that was in his hand. Then Esther went near and touched the top of the scepter. And the king said to her, "What do you wish, Queen Esther? What is your request? It shall be given to you—up to half the kingdom!" So Esther answered, "If it pleases the king, let the king and Haman come today to the banquet that I have prepared for him." Then the king said, "Bring Haman quickly, that he may do as Esther has said." So the king and Haman went to the banquet that Esther had prepared. At the banquet of wine the king said to Esther, "What is your petition? It shall be granted you. What is your request, up to half the kingdom? It shall be done!" Then Esther answered and said, "My petition and request is this: If I have found favor in the sight of the king, and if it pleases the king to grant my petition and fulfill my request, then let the king and Haman come to the banquet which I will prepare for them, and tomorrow I will do as the king has said." So Haman went out that day joyful and with a glad heart; but when Haman saw Mordecai in the king's gate, and that he did not stand or tremble before him, he was filled with indignation against Mordecai. Nevertheless Haman restrained himself and went home, and he sent and called for his friends **and his wife Zeresh.** Then Haman told them of his great riches, the multitude of his children, everything in

which the king had promoted him, and how he had advanced him above the officials and servants of the king. Moreover Haman said, "Besides, Queen Esther invited no one but me to come in with the king to the banquet that she prepared; and tomorrow I am again invited by her, along with the king. Yet all this avails me nothing, so long as I see Mordecai the Jew sitting at the king's gate." **Then his wife Zeresh and all his friends said to him, "Let a gallows be made, fifty cubits high, and in the morning suggest to the king that Mordecai be hanged on it; then go merrily with the king to the banquet."**

And the thing pleased Haman; so he had the gallows made (Esther 5:1-14, New King James Version).

I know that was a lot of reading, but don't you love this exciting book of the Bible? Did you notice the problem in this reading? His wife led him to do something evil, to plan to kill someone that didn't stroke her husband's ego. She ultimately planned the way her husband would die. Do you realize how impactful our words can be if we choose to speak negatively? Our husbands are leading God's people, and if we speak a word out of turn or with evil intention or motive, we could be prophesying death to our husbands and the ministry.

So let's pick up with the rest of the story.

Esther replied, "This wicked Haman is our adversary and our enemy." Haman grew pale with fright before the king and queen. Then the king jumped to his feet in a rage and went out into the palace garden. Haman, however, stayed behind to plead for his life with Queen Esther, for he knew that the king intended to kill him. In despair he fell on the couch where Queen Esther was reclining, just as the king was returning from the palace garden. The king exclaimed, "Will he even assault the queen right here in the palace, before my very eyes?" And as soon as the king spoke, his attendants covered Haman's face, signaling his doom. Then Harbona, one of the king's eunuchs, said, "Haman has set up a sharpened pole that stands seventy-five feet tall in his own courtyard. He intended to use it to impale Mordecai, the man who saved the king from assassination." So they impaled Haman on the pole he had set up for Mordecai, and the king's anger subsided (Esther 7:6-10, New Living Translation).

Our job, ladies, is to speak the truth in love and provide accountability. If we see or sense that something is getting out of hand within our husbands, we must pray and ask God how to bring this issue to our husband's attention.

Haman had a problem with pride, and we know that destruction is inevitable if left unchecked. So don't be like Haman's wife. She had a hunger for greed and power just like her husband did. It's quite possible that she made her husband the man that he had become because of her bad character.

An example of a leading lady that was willing to look out for her husband is Zipporah, Moses's wife. Do you remember in Exodus 4 when Moses was on his way to fulfill the Lord's command to lead His people out of Egypt? Let's look at this.

The Lord said to Moses in Midian, Go back to Egypt; for all the men who were seeking your life [for killing the Egyptian] are dead. And Moses took his wife and his sons and set them on donkeys, and he returned to the land of Egypt; and Moses took the rod of God in his hand. And the Lord said to Moses, When you return into Egypt, see that you do before Pharaoh all those miracles and wonders which I have put in your hand; but I will make him stubborn and harden his heart, so that he will not let the people go. And you shall say to Pharaoh, Thus says the Lord, Israel is My son, even My firstborn. And I say to you, Let My son go, that he may serve Me; and if you refuse to let him go, behold, I will slay your son, your firstborn. Along the way at a [resting-] place, the Lord met [Moses] and sought to kill him [made him acutely and almost fatally ill]. [Now apparently he had failed to circumcise one of his sons, his wife being opposed to it; but seeing his life in such danger] Zipporah took a flint knife and cut off the foreskin of her son and cast it to touch [Moses'] feet, and said, Surely a husband of blood you are to me! When He let [Moses] alone [to recover], Zipporah said, A husband of blood are you because of the circumcision (Exodus 4:19-26, Amplified).

Zipporah rose to the occasion and took care of what had been neglected. Apparently because of her culture, she didn't agree with Moses's culture to circumcise her son. At the point when her husband and ministry would have been destroyed, she stepped in and saved the day and did what needed to be done despite how she felt about it. That is exactly what we are called to do as a leading lady.

There are times when our husbands don't see the immediate need in the home and church because of the extreme pressure of ministry, and their focus is blurry. Moses was on the way to fulfill the heavenly mission, but there was one thing undone that could have cost him his life. Praise God for a wife that sees the small but important details and is willing to step up and make sure it gets done without disrespecting her husband. Theologians have much commentary on what this whole encounter meant, but at the end of all the debate – the leading lady saved the day!

Another great example of a leading lady speaking and reacting in the right way is Pilate's wife. In Matthew 27:19, she told Pilate to "leave that innocent man alone." Are you admonishing your husband? Are you being the helpmate that he needs? Are your words filled with wise counsel? Are your words seasoned with grace, love, and kindness? I'm stepping on my own toes now! Ouch! Help us all, Lord!

The worst thing we can do is fail to warn our spouses in advance and then say to them, "I knew this was going to happen." Ask God for discernment and wisdom to be a wife that will give timely advice in the correct manner. Ask God for insight into the matters of the church so that you can give the word of the Lord.

Leading Ladies Prayer for Wisdom and Discernment:

Father, I love you, and I love my husband. I desire for my husband to trust that what I speak is what You would say, and I want to do him good all the days of his life (Proverbs 31: 11). Forgive me for times that I have spoken idle words and acted selfishly when it comes to Your church. I want my husband to hear clearly from You about our family, our marriage, and ministry. Forgive me for causing him any distraction or confusion because of my misguided words. Give me the tongue of a disciple, that I should know how to speak a word in season to my husband when he is weary (Isaiah 50:4). May my words be filled with love, wisdom, and kindness. May You awaken me each day with an ear to hear what Holy Spirit is saying. Give me wisdom to know when and where and how to share whatever Holy Spirit says. In Jesus' name. Amen.

CHAPTER 8

REST

Definition of rest –

- Refreshing ease or inactivity after exertion or labor;
- Relief or freedom, especially from anything that wearies, troubles, or disturbs;
- Mental or spiritual calm
- Tranquility

This may be the most important chapter of this book. This four-letter word has been a reason for many of the problems that I have had in ministry. Lack of rest is an open door for the enemy to steal, kill, and destroy. As a leading lady, you and I must get adequate physical rest to not give the enemy place. You see, the enemy loves to attack our bodies with sickness. Most of the time, we get sick because we don't get enough rest.

When we're tired, we are also easily irritated and frustrated with ourselves and everyone else. Oh, the church might not know about our issue, but everyone close to us knows that we are in a mess. A downward spiral ensues until we hit the wall. My husband is and has been very frustrated because of my lack of ability to recognize when I'm exhausted. I tend to think that I'm resting, but his take on it is that I go take a nap when I've already hit the wall. I don't just take a day to check out and refresh physically. This is hard for us women to do, but I've had to force myself to take these resting vacations.

You see, the enemy doesn't care that you are winning souls and making headway. He tries to get you so tired that you can't continue, and then you become ineffective. I just recently experienced major victories. God used me mightily, but the days afterward were awful. I was so physically tired and easily agitated that I gave the enemy a place to push those closest to me away. I hope that these words are helping someone, because they are hard to write!

I tend to just keep wishing for a few days away to refresh on the beach or something, but the reality is that I don't have a few days at times. We took a five-day cruise, and it took three days for my mind to figure out that I was on vacation and that I could relax! The level of intensity and pressure that goes with our ministry is high, and it takes a while to detox.

You and I have to take moments of rest before we hit the wall. We must make time in our schedules for "me time." I'm stepping on my own toes. Hopefully, by me writing this book, it will hold me accountable. I'm tired of feeling like I just need to get away.

David felt the same way in Psalm 55 when he said, "Oh, that I had wings of a dove and I would fly away and be at rest." Reality is that we don't have wings. Calgon is not going to take us away! I know I just dated myself. But we need to find rest where we are at and be okay. Yes, vacations should be planned into our busy schedules. This is a must.

How many of us know that there are times when we don't see a break in the weekly schedule? Maybe just take a few hours on a Thursday. We have got to get our minds set on that time and make the most of it. Include your husband in your plans, because he needs rest too. He wants rest time with you. He wants to know that you have thought of him as well.

Here is the issue with a lack of rest. In Hebrews 4, we are reminded of the people of Israel in the wilderness. There was a huge number of them that didn't enter the promised place of blessing because of unbelief. They couldn't enter into the place of rest, because they didn't believe in the God that led them out of bondage.

As a leading lady, I have to keep reminding myself that God called us, and that He will have to be the One to do what He has told us to do. He will be the One to lead us into rest. Without Him, you and I can do nothing (John 15:5).

Most of the issues in the preceding chapters were caused by a lack of rest. It is imperative to rest. What is an activity or inactivity that enables you to feel like you've rested?

First of all, we need sleep. We need to go to bed early enough to sleep. This is easier said than done in ministry. If your schedule is like mine, there are some nights that we come home from either a wonderfully amazing day or a day that we felt like the wind was knocked out of us. We find ourselves having a hard time unwinding to go to sleep, so sometimes we sit down and watch something on TV to escape. Sometimes we will talk about the issue or rehearse the great happenings. This means we get to bed late and are sometimes overtired the next day, because we still toss and turn.

On those tossing and turning nights, my husband or I will get up and pray. The other one of us is also awake wondering if the other is okay. Needless to say, we sometimes end up tired the next day. As usual, we then have an early morning appointment or something going on, and we never recoup that rest.

If we have this type of spiritual weight and schedule for long periods of time, we will hit a brick wall (like I recently did). The pressure of what needed to be done and what I was responsible for got to me! I began to internalize the pressure, which is why I'm diagnosed with hypertension (which I'm believing to be healed from). I got this attitude of I don't care, and anyone that knows me knows that I'm not that type of person.

It's kind of hard to explain the dark cloud that I was under. What I do know is that the enemy loves to get us in this place of ineffectiveness, especially us ladies! If he can make us tired and lethargic, sick and tired of ministry, and negative and cranky toward our husbands, he has defeated us.

I thank God that my husband recognized that we were long overdue on just the two of us taking off. I believe I mentioned before that Raymond and I had a deal before we went into full time ministry, we would take off by ourselves every three months to refresh physically. Well, the last time we intentionally went off during was over five months, and I had pretty much had a meltdown. It was so bad that I didn't go to praise team rehearsal, because I just didn't want this junk to rub off on anyone or rub anyone the wrong way. My poor husband was already getting rubbed the wrong way.

Like I was saying, my husband got the hint. We escaped and went to my favorite place in the world with sand and water…the ocean. There is something about the smell and sound of the ocean that puts me where I need to be physically and emotionally.

The money that you spend to get away is worth it, so don't allow that to be an excuse. In fact, don't use any excuse. Just do it, even if it's you that has to do the planning. Sometimes, I am the one to plan our getaway. A lot of times, my husband doesn't even realize that he's burned out. But every time we go off he'll say, "I didn't know I needed to get away, and I'm so glad we did!" Most of the reason he is excited when we get away is because I'm a better wife, friend, and lover to him when I'm rested.

You and I are anointed to help our husbands be relaxed. How do men relax? They do this by spending quality, intimate time with us. Ladies, that is why we must rest. If we aren't rested, we won't be able to take care of our husbands' needs. Remember, our mission in life according to the Word of God, is to be his helpmeet (to help him meet his destiny). He can't meet his destiny if we aren't in the right place physically, emotionally, and spiritually.

I also want to encourage you to be creative in your intimate relationship with your husband. Your husband is a man first. We live in this flesh, and men need physical intimacy! Even more so, he needs this as a spiritual leader. The pressure or weight that your man of God is under is indescribable. He needs his physical needs met, so it will not become an added pressure for him.

How do we stay rested and in the right place for ourselves and for our man of God? There are five areas of R. E. S. T. that will keep us in our optimal place for optimal success.

1. Relationship Established in Sanctifying Truth- We must make sure that our relationship with Christ is firmly grounded in the sanctifying and cleansing Word of God. Our worth and self-esteem must be rooted in what the Word of God says about us and not how we feel. We cannot afford to be easily intimidated or offended in ministry. If we know who we are, we can behave accordingly. The Word of God will wash us and keep us set apart for the Master's use. If you need accountability in staying in the Word, get with another leading lady that you may be pouring into and start a devotion together. The YouVersion Bible app makes it incredibly easy to connect and use for accountability.

2. Refreshed Exclusively by the Savior's Touch - We must know how to get into our Savior's presence and how to be touched by the Lover of our soul at any time. You see, there are times when

my husband doesn't pick up on the fact that I need him. There are times when he's so emotionally and spiritually spent that he doesn't have anything to give, and he's looking for me to be there for him. We've had times that we were hit with a hard blow, like having a choir member sleeping with the choir director's husband or when the married drummer is having inappropriate relationship with underage girls in the church. What do you do? Or what about when your own child is bound up by the enemy? You better know how to get into the presence of the Lord and how to be refreshed by Him alone. It's sad when you hear of a pastor's wife that is addicted to pills or posts on Facebook that they are feeling depressed. Be quick to go boldly to the throne of grace to find mercy and grace to help in the time of need (Hebrews 4:16). You may have to get up earlier than everyone in the house to have your time. You may need to go walking and spend that time in prayer. You may need to lay in the church altar several times a week just being quiet in the Father's presence. Whatever it takes, because our lives depend on it. Times of refreshing come from the presence of the Lord (Acts 3:19).

3. Relaxed Entirely in His Supernatural Tendencies – We must remember that God is God, and He does things supernaturally. We cannot rest if we are worried about the church, the money (or lack of), the kids, and the list goes on! We have got to believe that He will provide and guide us supernaturally no matter what. He took care of the children of Israel for 40 years in the wilderness. He protected, guided, and fed them supernaturally! How much more now that we are bought with the precious blood of Jesus will He take care of us? We are His daughters! Besides, He called us. He chose us. As long as we follow His directions, we can relax. Right? Initially, I wrote this a while ago; but, even as I go through and am reading this again, I'd like to add that just last week I had to lay ministry at the foot of the cross and remind myself once again that this is His church and not mine. I can't stress out about the ministry that He placed me in. It's His. I have to always remember that ministry can end

today, but my relationship with Jesus is eternal and my marriage will last our lifetime. With that said, I am going to choose to focus my eyes on what will last for eternity and trust Him for everything else.

4. Receive Education from Spiritual Teachers – This is a big one. Very few people in ministry have someone that is pouring into them, someone that they trust can speak into their life. Unfortunately, there are ministers that don't feel they need this, because they think they know it all. The Word says that leaders are to be teachable. You can safely rest if we just listen to those who have gone before us. They will give us good instruction that will help us to be better women of God. Ask God to show you who would be that mentor and confidante. Don't try to be a girlfriend to those you lead. Yes, be open and approachable, but be careful to not be too familiar. If you do this, they won't listen when you need to speak into their life. The Lord will give you someone outside of your church that can give you an unbiased and godly response to a personal or ministry issue. He may give

you different women for different issues. Just make sure that your husband agrees with the women that you confide in so that he can trust them, too.

5. Realize Eternity Supersedes Today – Keep the main thing the main thing! We are to be focused on eternity and not on temporary things. We can rest if we know that this world is not our home (Hebrews 13:14). We must stay focused on leading others to make a decision for eternity. Nothing else matters but hearing the Father say, "Well done, my good and faithful servant" (Matthew 25:23). Let's not be so concerned with self, but let's fulfill the heavenly vision. Be available for your husband in ministry. Be faithful to help him fulfill the mission that God put you together to accomplish.

And Jesus came and spoke to them, saying, "All authority has been given to Me in heaven and on earth. Go therefore and make disciples of all the nations, baptizing them in the name of the Father and of the Son and of the Holy Spirit, teaching them to observe all things that I have commanded you; and lo, I am with you always, even to the end of the age." Amen (Matthew 28:19-20, New King James Version).

We can rest in knowing that no matter what, Jesus will be with us always, even to the end of the age!

Leading Ladies Prayer for Rest:

Father, first of all, I ask You to forgive me for not living in the rest that You have provided. Father, I receive Your rest. There is no other place that I want to be but in Your perfect will. Please forgive me for taking the ministry responsibilities into my own hands and not allowing You to guide me just like a child. This is too big for me, but I know that You are big and strong enough to handle each task. I want to rest in you and allow You to lead me beside the still waters (Psalm 23:2). You know what's best for me, and You know how to make me lie down in green pastures. Father, I don't want You to have to make me lie down, rather, I choose to lie down. You are so good. I want to be a Leading Lady that leads others to those green pastures, and I know that can only happen if I'm rested. Help me to make this a priority and schedule weekly rest time so that I'm more God-centered than self-centered. In Jesus' name. Amen.

CHAPTER 9

REAL TALK – UNCUT & UNEDITED

The following are encouraging nuggets that just talk about practical application and situations that Leading Ladies will face or need to consider.

Betrayal

You WILL be betrayed by the one closest to you. 1 out of 12 people will turn out to be a traitor. Keep your heart open and vulnerable regardless. A guarded heart in leadership is a compromised heart. When you need to minister, you will hold back because of fear of being hurt again. Vulnerability and being quick to forgive is a must or you will be easy prey for the enemy.

Let the Lord Take Over

I have some good news for you! You don't have to protect yourself! You don't have to open your mouth to prove anything. If you've been blamed and misunderstood, humble yourself, ask the person for forgiveness and let it go. Trust me, you will be misunderstood and blamed as a leading lady. The enemy will always come after the leading lady to attempt to shut you down. Don't take it personal. Know that you are powerful and there is greatness in you that your adversary wants to silence and paralyze. So, stand still and see the salvation of the Lord. Be still and know that He is God. Know that the battle is the Lord's and there's no need to fight. The Lord says to you, "Vengeance is Mine, I will repay." Keep your heart open and your mouth shut!

Relax and Release

Allow others to help you and don't redo what they try to do. Train them and release them. The worse thing we can do is make other women feel like they don't know what they are doing if we come behind them and do it all over again. Work on clearly communicating your desire and then release people. If it's not done the way you would have done it, it's okay. Others will only get better if they practice. We all have to start somewhere. Ministry will be a chore for us unless we train and release. Remember Pastor Raymond's 3T Principle - Touch with Love. Teach with Care. Train with Passion. I don't want to be a leading lady that no one wants to work with. I know you don't either.

Overwhelmed?

Are you overwhelmed? The definition of overwhelm according to Dictionary.com is to be overcome completely in mind or feeling, to be buried or covered by a mass of something. We can be positively or negatively overwhelmed. Which one are you? There is an occasion to be overwhelmed by circumstances of which you have no control. "I sink in deep mire, where there is no foothold; I have come into deep waters, where the floods overwhelm me." Psalm 69:2 AMP

Maybe you feel overwhelmed because of the arrows of the enemy that he's constantly shooting your way and you're getting weary. "For the enemy has pursued and persecuted my soul, he has crushed my life down to the ground; he has made me to dwell in dark places as those who have been long dead. Therefore is my spirit overwhelmed and faints within me [wrapped in gloom]; my heart within my bosom grows numb." Psalm 143:3-4 AMP

What do we do if we feel overwhelmed for whatever reason? We cry out to our Father! Be still and allow Him to overwhelm us in His love. The good kind of overwhelmed.

"From the end of the earth will I cry to You, when my heart is overwhelmed and fainting; lead me to the rock that is higher than I [yes, a rock that is too high for me]."

Psalm 61:2 AMP

Honestly, I'm overwhelmed right now. It was a negative type of overwhelmed up until yesterday. I was allowing myself to be buried in the tasks given to me. But then I realized something. I need to be thankful and glorify God for this task that is BIGGER THAN ME. It's beyond me and my capabilities. It's My Father's opportunity to shine, not mine.

As a leading lady, there will be times of feeling overwhelmed, but I pray that we quickly refocus that feeling to know our Daddy says, "When you pass through the waters, I will be with you, and through the

rivers, they will not overwhelm you. When you walk through the fire, you will not be burned or scorched, nor will the flame kindle upon you."
Isaiah 43:2 AMP

Let us be overwhelmed by His love and not with the affairs of this life! "He brought me to the banqueting house, and his banner over me was love [for love waved as a protecting and comforting banner over my head when I was near him]."
Song of Solomon 2:4 AMP

Balance

The word I hear in my spirit this morning is BALANCE. The definition of balance is mental steadiness or emotional stability; habit of calm behavior, judgment, etc. OR equal distribution of weight, amount, etc. How do we balance it all? The only way we can stay balanced is to make time for rest.

I stretch myself out. I sleep. Then I'm up again—rested, tall and steady, Fearless before the enemy mobs Coming at me from all sides. (Psalm 3:5-6 MSG).

"In peace I will both lie down and sleep, for You, Lord, alone make me dwell in safety and confident trust."

Psalm 4:8 AMP

"He makes me lie down in [fresh, tender] green pastures; He leads me beside the still and restful waters."

Psalm 23:2 AMP

It's amazing what happens when I've awaken from a nap! I think clearer and my body is relaxed. Don't let the enemy tell you that you don't have time to rest. If Jesus the author and the finisher of our faith took time to rest we need to as well. His ministry was 24/7, under death threats and had a constant demand for His attention. We cannot imagine what it was like but He amazingly gave us a great example of withdrawing from the crowd and resting. We need to stay rested so we can have plenty of energy for our husbands so we are ready for them emotionally, spiritually and physically. Remember to keep them a high priority. I'm reminding myself of this too!

Priorities

How have you been doing balancing it all this week? Just want to encourage you to prioritize your husband as you do ministry and everything else. Make him feel like he is more important than anything and anyone else besides Jesus. If Jesus is our priority, Holy Spirit will lead us to make our husbands needs a priority. Be available for him physically. He needs your attention because although they are men they are only as strong and focused as we are. Take time out of your week, make plans for the kids , buy something sexy or not. You know what your husband likes. Don't let your marriage get all ho hum and boring. Keep it spicy!

"Let marriage be held in honor (esteemed worthy, precious, of great price, and especially dear) in all things. And thus let the marriage bed be undefiled (kept undishonored);...

Hebrews 13:4 AMP

Overtaken

I was overtaken with some junk in my mind yesterday. I found myself off track. Earlier that day in my spirit, I heard Joshua 1:8 to meditate on the Word and I'll make my own way prosperous and I'll have good success. Also to be very careful with my words...to only say what I hear from the Father. Well, I failed throughout the rest of the day and I found my husband and I not on one accord. I fell into a trap. I stopped meditating on the good things. Exactly what I had preached on Wednesday! Don't think we won't be tested on what we preach to others. So today I hear the scriptures in I Peter 5:8-11 and I like how the Message version puts it and I had to share because 9 times out of 10 it will encourage you too. "Keep a cool head. Stay alert. The Devil is poised to pounce and would like nothing better than to catch you napping. Keep your guard up. You're not the only ones plunged into these hard times. It's the same with Christians all over the world. So keep a firm grip on the faith. The suffering won't last forever. It won't be long before this generous God who has great plans for us in Christ—

eternal and glorious plans they are!—will have you put together and on your feet for good. He gets the last word; yes, he does."

1 Peter 5:8-11 MSG

Thank you for allowing me to be open and honest with you! I have POWER, LOVE and a SOUND MIND! #striving #pressing

Joy is a Necessity

"You will show me the path of life; in Your presence is fullness of joy, at Your right hand there are pleasures forevermore."

Psalm 16:11 AMP

Are you having full joy? Don't live on fumes. The enemy's trick is to get us so busy that we keep ministering and going without the fullness of joy. Then we get weak and break. We get weak and break because we lose the joy! The Lords joy gives us STRENGTH! Therefore, we have to stay full of joy by staying in His presence! No weak leading ladies here! We are strong and full of joy in Jesus name!

Big Ministry Requires Stronger Marriages

We have heard so many times in our services that what's coming is BIG! Sunday night I heard in my spirit that BIGGER ministry requires STRONGER MARRIAGES! If we aren't fulfilling our husband's fantasies, being aggressive and not passive, letting him know how desirable he is, we will give an open door to the enemy. Remember Pastor Rhonda said the anointing is attractive. Your husband might not look like Matthew McConaughey but believe me that somebody wants him when he's flowing in the anointing. Women are attracted to men of God. We must be creative! Keep the sex relationship fun and exciting! Yandy.com is a great place to get some inspiration. Don't wait for him to approach you.. Playing the "who will touch each other first" game. Start thinking about sex early in the day so we can get our minds and bodies ready. Men know if we are just going through the motions. Make sure he's sees your naked body. Your image needs to be burned into his memory. Get over your self consciousness. Your husband loves you, all of you! I can talk about this all day because this was a battle in our marriage for many years. If you can't perform that night for whatever reason, don't wait till he thinks he's gonna get some once he's in the bed and then tell him you can't. Tell him way before then. Ok now I'm gonna sound like your mom. (Count it as a reminder if you know these things. My mom didn't teach me this stuff.) Go to bed with a clean and fresh body. Wear or don't wear what your husband likes. Wash your bed sheets weekly and keep your bed fresh. Don't talk about ministry in the bedroom. Don't talk about ministry all the time either. Talk about you and your husband. Ministry can end tomorrow, but marriage lasts forever so keep it in perspective. If you have questions, I'm more than happy to share with you a few things I have learned in my marriage and in counseling sessions with other couples through the years. BIGGER MINISTRY REQUIRES STRONGER MARRIAGES.

Fearless

Leading Ladies are FEARLESS! "They (the righteous) are confident and fearless and can face their foes triumphantly."
Psalms 112:8 NLT

"I'm proud to praise God, proud to praise GOD. Fearless now, I trust in God; what can mere mortals do to me?"

Psalm 56:10-11 MSG

"....I'm fearless, afraid of no one and nothing." Psalm 27:1 MSG

"For God has not given us a spirit of fear and timidity, but of power, love, and self-discipline."

2 Timothy 1:7 NLT

    Don't allow other women and their actions to cause you to back away from them, avoid them and cause you to separate from them. Can women rub you wrong? Can they rub others wrong? Absolutely! I'd rather get close to the woman who leaves destruction in her path than to allow the weaker ones to be affected. So as a Leading Lady don't run from the unlovable. Run to them and ask Holy Spirit about how to minister to this woman who is obviously hurting because she hurts others. If you run from the "hard to deal with" woman you will always be running because there is one or two in EVERY CHURCH! Trust me. So be fearless knowing that your Father goes before you and you can face any enemy! In your prayer time, take authority over that foul spirit that is tormenting that woman. Be bold, be fearless! Be strong in the Lord and in the power of HIS might!

Encourage Your Man

Get your pom-poms out and be a cheerleader to your husband. Your husband needs to hear you encouraging him on a regular basis. Not just encouraging him in the ministry but also as a man. Make him feel desirable by telling him how sexy he is and how much you desire him. Now I have to tell you that I struggled with telling my husband these things because I thought I sounded stupid and not sexy. I had to get past my flesh and begin to do it for him. Don't let others tell your husband how good your husband looks and how wonderful he is. Be the first to encourage him. "Therefore encourage (admonish, exhort) one another and edify (strengthen and build up) one another...."

1 Thessalonians 5:11 AMP

Plan Ahead

"If we fail to plan, we plan to fail." It's officially summer break and many things are going on around us but my encouragement to us this week is to be careful to plan. Plan ahead. Now we just can't plan anything that pops into our head. As leading ladies, we must spend time in the presence of the Lord to get a download of what He wants us to do. "Roll your works upon the Lord [commit and trust them wholly to Him; He will cause your thoughts to become agreeable to His will, and] so shall your plans be established and succeed."
Proverbs 16:3 AMP

Then we submit what Holy Spirit is telling us to our heads, our husbands, our priests. "Wives, submit yourselves unto your own husbands, as unto the Lord."
Ephesians 5:22 KJV

This goes for our ministries and well as our personal lives. I can't tell you how many times I've failed in this area. I've made plans without consulting my head and this caused major chaos and confusion in my relationship. Our primary goal should be a help and not a hindrance to our husbands in our marriage and ministry. So plan as your pray and pray as you plan. May our husbands know that when we speak that we've heard from heaven! Be careful to plan to spend time with your husband. Sometimes we plan for everyone and everything else but we don't prioritize our marriage. This is a must to maintain your relationship and be in full time ministry. Make your husband feel that you thought about him FIRST.

"May He grant you according to your heart's desire and fulfill all your plans."

Psalm 20:4 AMP

Discipline

In June 2016, I was blessed to graduate from Life Christian University with a Bachelor of Arts Degree in Theology in Tampa, Florida! Glory to God! This has been a dream that has taken 18 years to see in the natural! What are dreaming to accomplish? Whatever your dream is that you want to see, it's going to require DISCIPLINE. I had to discipline myself to FINISH! My husband tells me if I won't discipline myself and line up with the vision and what my pastor/husband is saying in spiritual and natural areas, the body (the church) won't either. As we all know, everything flows down. If the heads out of whack, the body will be too. If we have a lack of discipline in our life as a Leading Lady, the church will too! Now I'm not talking about religious bondage. No, I hate religion! I'm talking about the small things that Holy Spirit has told us to do or not do that we haven't disciplined ourselves in. You know it's the "little foxes that spoil the vine." (Song of Solomon 2:15)

Those little things that we let slide and have not been obedient to do can cause major damage in the long run. For me, it's not texting or emailing before reading and praying in the mornings, only getting on Facebook between the hours of 12-5 pm, not eating after 7 pm, etc. Again, that's a few I have disciplined myself in. That's me. We must take inventory and see where we lack discipline and discipline ourselves. It may seem insignificant but making these adjustments can affect the magnitude of the ministry that the Father has for me. Disciples are disciplined! The Lord is wanting to know if He can trust us with BIG things He has for us! The things that others think is okay to do or say or partake is not acceptable for a Leading Lady. Leading Ladies keep eternity in focus while walking submitted to her husband as unto the Lord!

I'm reminded of this scripture, "But [like a boxer] I buffet my body [handle it roughly, discipline it by hardships] and subdue it, for fear that after proclaiming to others the Gospel and things pertaining to it, I myself should become unfit [not stand the test, be unapproved and rejected as a counterfeit]."
1 Corinthians 9:27 AMP. I don't want to be called a counterfeit! Let's be obedient to the prompting of Holy Spirit in areas in which we need to tighten up so the Father will know we are ready for the BIG things He has in store for us! Not only that, we can't require discipline from those under our leadership if we aren't disciplined in our daily lives. Love you dearly and have a beautiful day!

Forgiveness

Leading Ladies quickly forgive people before they even know they need forgiveness.

"And he came up to Jesus at once and said, Hail (greetings, good health to You, long life to You), Master! And he embraced Him and kissed Him with [pretended] warmth and devotion." Matthew 26:49 AMP

As you well know it was Judas that kissed Jesus and pretended to be warm and devoted after he had sold him out for thirty pieces of silver. It was the one who dipped his hand in the cup at the same time Jesus did. The one who had wrong motives and thoughts about Jesus. The one of the twelve that Jesus spent 3 1/2 years with.

I want to share with you a sad reality that you WILL be betrayed as a Leading Lady! Most of the time by the one closest to you in ministry! The one you ministered to the most. You WILL be criticized and misunderstood! You WILL be accused of things that you did or didn't do! I'm sure most of you have figured it out. The enemy comes after the Leading Lady most of the time because he knows that if he can get us all bound up with junk, we will infect our husbands and then ultimately destroy the ministry.

One of our mentors always says, "Your ministry will only go as high as the criticism you are willing to take." Let that sink in for a moment. So does that mean to be passive and cower down to the women in your ministry? Does that mean to hide from being who you need to be as you serve alongside your husband? Does that mean to be afraid to reach out to women? ABSOLUTELY NOT! The enemy is wanting us to be passive, fearful and hide. You know what that does? It prevents us from impacting the women that need the treasures on the inside of us! It keeps us from being available when our husbands need us because we don't want to be involved.

    I've always had at least one woman that consistently bucks everything I do while pretending to be warm and devoted. What I've learned is that my job is to stay submitted to my husband in everything at home and church and to keep leading and loving. I'm going to keep having joy and not allow the hurt on the inside of others to affect or infect me. There are way too many women who need us to be open, transparent, loving and approachable. Your women need you!

If you've been wounded by the women you're leading, forgive QUICKLY! Their issue is NOT your issue! This past week we got a Facebook message from a person who left our church not long after we became the pastors and had said all kinds of things about us and the church, begging for forgiveness because she is in need of a miracle now and wants to get things right. We forgave them a LONG TIME ago. Harboring unforgiveness is bondage.

Ladies, our husbands need us to be positive about ministry. We pull them down by talking about Sis. Sour Patch at home. (We have a rule to not talk about ministry at home and especially not in our bedroom.) Get in your prayer closet and cry out to the Father about Sis. Sour Patch not your husband! Let Him deal with her while you ask Holy Spirit for a way to love on her. Stay in that closet till you can embrace the rough ones and mean it from your heart. Keep your heart open and forgive quickly! Share your experiences with dealing the Sis.

Sour Patches, overcoming betrayal and hurt in ministry, valuable lessons you have learned, etc.

Is Your Receiver Broken?

I pray you've had a great week of forgiving people quickly! There is so much freedom in just letting it go, isn't it?

Well, I haven't been able to get away from two words this week HUMILITY and TEACHABLE. Are we humble enough to be taught? "A scoffer seeks Wisdom in vain [for his very attitude blinds and deafens him to it], but knowledge is easy to him who [being teachable] understands."
Prov. 14:6 AMP

As Leading Ladies, we spend a great deal of time encouraging and teaching others but who do we receive from? (I'm humbled that you'd take time to read my little devotion!) Holy Spirit can speak to us through anything and anyone. The scripture above said that our very attitude can blind and deafen us to receiving wisdom. So the question is what is our attitude when someone tries to teach or share something with us? Are we open to receive from the least likely sources? My daughter taught me a lot through the years, especially helped me to loosen up! I greatly value her opinion on spiritual and natural issues. The Lord has given her such wisdom! I'm also open to hear from other Leading Ladies who might have been in ministry for a shorter time than I have. I'm blessed with several mentors that I can reach out to and they give me scriptural advice, not their opinion. These ladies are not in my church, not even in my state. (The people you lead can't be your friends. You might be wondering why...We can talk more about that next week.) You need a woman that you can believe her motives are pure and you can receive from. There is always something to glean from others. My pastor used to say, "Eat the meat and throw away the bones!"

Most importantly, are you humble to receive from your husband, your priest? Not receiving from your priest is a reflection of not receiving from the Lord. (Eph. 5:22) In my case, my husband is my pastor and my boss because I serve as the worship pastor. It is difficult at times to not blur the lines. We make it a general rule to schedule ministry appointments in the office to keep our ministry relationship professional and respectful. It's so easy for me to slip into wife mode! I have to make a conscious effort to humble myself and receive criticism and correction from him in the ministry. Learning how to humble myself and to be teachable has been key for me and my husband to flow in ministry together. Lord, help us as Leading Ladies to stay humble and teachable! Please share your insights in humility and being teachable to help us all. Love you!

Healthy Friendships

As I shared last week, I will talk about why it's not the best idea for a Leading Lady to have friends in her church. What do I mean by friends? When I say "friend", I mean a woman that you can share your victories, struggles, frustrations in ministry and just keep it real! That friend needs to be from outside the church (so they can be unbiased) and mature enough to hear you, love you and still believe you are anointed and called. They need to be able to allow you to talk it out and (if necessary) encourage you to get back in the fight and let it go. The need for having friends to be right up under you needs to be healed in ministry. I think first we need to ask ourselves the question, why do we feel we need friends in the church. The reality is this, how can you be friends with a sheep? You and your husband are called to lead sheep. The women in your church need you to lead because they want an example to follow. How can we speak the Word of the Lord into their lives when they feel you know too much about them? Many people don't know how to keep the boundaries and respect your position because they have gotten too familiar with you.

    We have Holy Spirit to comfort and guide us and He should be the first Person we run to. Then we have our awesome husbands. My husband is my best friend and I can talk with him about anything. He is also my pastor! There are times when I need to get something off my chest but he's not able to just let me vent depending on how deep the situation is. (Please note: The woman that you share with needs to be someone that your husband/pastor is in agreement with.) Remember, men process differently than we do. They process internally and we process by talking. You need someone that you can get it out with and it goes no further. You need someone that can tell you when you're wrong. "Iron sharpens iron; so a man sharpens the countenance of his friend [to show rage or worthy purpose]." (Proverbs 27:17 AMP) You need someone you can let your hair down with. A person that you may only talk with a few times a year but it's still a deep relationship. When you get together, it's like you pick up right where you left off. "Oil and perfume rejoice the heart; so does the sweetness of a friend's counsel that comes from the heart." (Proverbs 27:9 AMP)

I see so many lonely and guarded pastors/ministers wives. Most of the time, they've gotten that way because they were wounded by someone in the church that they thought was their friend. Ask the Father to connect you with someone that you can share with. I have two ladies primarily in my life that I deeply love and respect that I'm able to call on. I have one In my life for leadership issues and wisdom and another when I need to just get some things out personally and then we preach to each other! Lol!

This week we have a dear pastoral couple visiting with us from Washington State. We talk with them about everything. I can share with the wife about my frustrations, struggles and what the Lord is speaking. We preach to each other! I haven't seen her for almost two years but it's like we saw each other last month! We talk and text a couple of times throughout the year and it's always refreshing and encouraging. She understands the position as a leading lady. I absolutely love, love, love, my ladies at my church and I am deeply connected to the five pastors wives that I lead in my church. I want my pastors wives to be able to come to me with their frustrations and struggles in ministry and also personally. I need that person in my life as well. I hope you hear my heart that it's important that we have someone (like a David & Jonathan relationship) that you can let your hair down with. I'd love to hear your thoughts about this topic. Do you have a David & Jonathan relationship in your life? If not, why?

Free to Testify

This week I've been meeting a lot with women and one in particular said that she felt like she needed to tell me about what she done in her past because she might not want be welcome in our church if we knew. She felt like she couldn't go any further before she got it out and could be completely open. When she shared it, I just smiled because I had not only done it myself but I had done it three times! When I shared my testimony with her, a great wave of peace and relief washed all over her. What if I was still walking in shame and condemnation? What if I wasn't free to share my yuck? As a Leading Lady, it is imperative that we receive forgiveness and freedom from our past so that we can freely testify when needed. When others can see you walk in joy and freedom knowing you have overcome some huge hurdles, they gain confidence that Jesus will use them to do great things too. Praise God that I don't look like what I've been through. Be open when Holy Spirit prompts you to share because unfortunately people don't believe we've had a pre-Jesus time in our life unless we share it! Your testimony will set others free and give them hope that she could be a Leading Lady one day!

Be the Same No Matter What

As I am away at General Assembly this week, a biennial event for the Church of God denomination, I am reminded again of a key truth for a successful, long ministry. Here it is, ladies. Don't lose yourself in your position, in your ministry because ministry and positions will change. I'm watching the process of positions being transferred to others. Ministries and responsibilities will change rapidly for many. I think about the many Leading Ladies that will need to pack and move their lives to a new state and position or to no position at all. (I really don't want to be one of those who come to General Assembly and then my whole life changes!) Talk about being nervous. Regardless, if and when ministry and positions change, (because they will) I pray that my identity remain intact. The definition of identity is the state of remaining the SAME under varying aspects or conditions; the condition of being oneself. We are called and gifted to do ministry but at the end of the day and when I stand before Jesus, I'm Lorna. If the title or position were stripped today, who am I without position? Who are you without position? Are we the same regardless? I pray that our

relationship with Jesus is so vibrant and passionate that we would find our identity in Him and our mission to fulfill the Great Commission. "For we are God's [own] handiwork (His workmanship), recreated in Christ Jesus, [born anew] that we may do those good works which God predestined (planned beforehand) for us [taking paths which He prepared ahead of time], that we should walk in them [living the good life which He prearranged and made ready for us to live]."
Ephesians 2:10 AMP

Leading Ladies are secure in their identity aside from position. Relax. Be yourself. Have fun. Something I have to remind myself of daily! I think the greatest example we can display to others is to be authentic as a Leading Lady.

It's Me, Oh Lord, Standing in the Need of Prayer

It's transparency day! You know I sometimes find myself looking at the faults of others in my church family more than my own. (I know you don't do this.) Have you ever sat down to read your Bible and come across a scripture that reminds you of a situation in the church?

Then your mind goes straight to that person who really needs that Word? Then you maybe send them that scripture, right? Well that's good thing but our whole devotion time can get consumed with thinking that "sister so and so" needs this and then we neglect ourselves from allowing the Word to wash us. (Again, I may just be talking about myself today.) It's so easy to become consumed with issues in the lives of the families we lead. This week I've been focusing on humility. News flash! I can't change me! Nor can I change anyone else so my focus should be to stay humble realizing that if not for the grace of God I could be dealing with that situation or issue. I have my own issues! One of those issues that I have to put to death daily is being critical. As a Leading Lady, we can easily slip into being critical or fault finding. We have people in our congregations that cause problems, are not faithful, give our husbands/pastors and children a hard time, won't listen to us when we spend our time advising, etc. It's easy to get prideful and critical but I'm reminded of I Corinthians 13:7 which says "Love bears up under anything and everything that comes, is ever ready to believe the best of every person, its hopes are fadeless under all circumstances, and it endures everything [without weakening]." Lord help me not get prideful or critical because at one time I too was blinded to how my actions were affecting and infecting others.

"Clothe (apron) yourselves, all of you, with humility [as the garb of a servant, so that its covering cannot possibly be stripped from you, with freedom from pride and arrogance] toward one another. For God sets Himself against the proud (the insolent, the overbearing, the disdainful, the presumptuous, the boastful)–[and He opposes, frustrates, and defeats them], but gives grace (favor, blessing) to the humble. Therefore humble yourselves [demote, lower yourselves in your own estimation] under the mighty hand of God, that in due time He may exalt you, Casting the whole of your care [all your anxieties, all your worries, all your concerns, once and for all] on Him, for He cares for you affectionately and cares about you watchfully."

1 Peter 5:5b-7 AMP

As a Leading Lady we've got to quickly cast our cares and humble ourselves in prayer about those issues that get us in our "feelings."

"For everyone who exalts himself will be humbled (ranked below others who are honored or rewarded), and he who humbles himself (keeps a modest opinion of himself and behaves accordingly) will be exalted (elevated in rank)."

Luke 14:11 AMP

Leading Ladies walk in humility.

Wait for It

Timing is everything! Those three words have been the key to success in ministry and when not heeded they have been the reason for strife in marriage & ministry. As a Leading Lady, we see issues that need to be fixed, addressed and confronted. I don't know about you but I tend to want things changed yesterday! Especially when divisive people are involved. Ive learned that it doesn't work like that. (I've got the scars to prove it.) Many times I have weighted my husband down with my thoughts, opinions and concerns only to make him feel more stressed. Then there are times when I'm 100% right but I start talking to my husband about it at the wrong time. Oh yes, I have also said the right thing but in the wrong tone and my husband felt like I'm bossing him around.

There is "a time to keep silence, and a time to speak;" Ecclesiastes 3:7b ESV

We definitely hear from God and the Lord shows us things for a reason! The reason is so we can pray! Our voice is important to our husbands but we must "flesh out" what the Lord is showing us in prayer so when we speak we are speaking the Word of the Lord. When we speak out of turn, it will immediately rub our husbands the wrong way. Ladies, when I have really spent time talking to the Lord about it, my husband readily receives from me.

Whoever speaks, [let him do it as one who utters] oracles of God; .... so that in all things God may be glorified through Jesus Christ (the Messiah). To Him be the glory and dominion forever and ever (through endless ages). Amen (so be it).

1 Peter 4:11 AMP

A word fitly spoken and in due season is like apples of gold in settings of silver. Proverbs 25:11 AMP

Father, help us to mindful of our concerns to our husbands. That we yield to Holy Spirit to give us the right time, words and tone so that we will be received. May our words carry the weight of your glory! Help us to go to You first! We declare peace in our marriages and ministries. In Jesus name.

LEADING LADIES WAIT ON THE TIMING OF THE LORD.

Guard Your Heart (Part 1)

As Leading Ladies, we obviously have to deal with people. People who may blatantly rebel against your husband or your leadership. You may hear about what they've said or hear it yourself! Holy Spirit may show you the condition of their heart is in your prayer time.

In our ministry we have inherited leaders. Leaders that were already in a position but very quickly we found out their motives were wrong. Attitudes, murmuring and complaining that they had would get back to us. I can't tell you that encountering these situations hasn't bothered me. It does. It's very easy to dwell on the negative but what does that get me? It will cause me to be a bitter pastors wife. That's the last thing we need.. another bitter pastors wife. So I want to encourage us all to GUARD OUR HEARTS.

"Keep and guard your heart with all vigilance and above all that you guard, for out of it flow the springs of life." Proverbs 4:23 AMP

If the situation and people involved consume our mind.. thinking about what they said all the time, we are in danger of a root of bitterness. It's time to stop everything and lay before the Lord and cry out to Him. Forgive and release these people realizing we don't wrestle against flesh and blood. (Ephesians 6:12) Be honest with your Father. He knows how much you think about it. He knows you have a problem with how they treated you and your family. He knows it hurts so say it to Him. "Lord, this hurts!" Lay it all on the table so you can be free! I had to do this this morning! I tossed and turned all night about several things. Do not fret or have any anxiety about anything, but in every circumstance and in everything, by prayer and petition (definite requests), with thanksgiving, continue to make your wants known to God. And God's peace [shall be yours, that tranquil state of a soul assured of its salvation through Christ, and so fearing nothing from God and being content with its earthly lot of whatever sort that is, that peace] which transcends all understanding shall garrison and mount guard over your hearts and minds in Christ Jesus. Philippians 4:6-7 AMP

    I want to stay free so I can love the ones who are ready to receive! So guard your heart from taking in any bitterness. I like to really open up to you all about real things that I deal with. I hope it helps you!

Guard Your Heart (Part II)

You know sometimes we can read and study and always have a word for everyone else? Neglecting ourselves? Really deceiving ourselves. I realized last week that I had really just gotten extremely negative. My husband kept calling me out on it but I wouldn't take it seriously but some old habits of interrupting him and disrespecting him were popping up too much and there was something wrong. The Father told me that I had lost my focus on loving Him by loving the hard to love people. We are supposed to love the hard to love people in our ministries. Even the ones who kick against our husband's vision. Even the ones who refuse to get with the program! I had become resentful. I had let resentment against people in leadership. The Father told me that I had neglected my heart. That thorns and thistles had begun to grow up and choke the word, the love out. He said that was why all I could see was the negative. Have you been there? Are you there now? The Father gave me three key scriptures that I have stopped everything to focus on. More than once a day looking into this mirror. I no longer want to be one who looks in the mirror and sees the booger and then walk away and forget. I want to faithfully persevere in this mirror so the Word can wash me. He led me to Luke 6:27-48, I Corinthians 13, and James 1:21-27.

I've ended up sharing the revelations with several over the last few days and I'm not the only one that's dealing with this. I got alone with the Father on last Tuesday and repented of my hard heartedness. Then I began to pray for those who I had become resentful against. What is resentment? The feeling of displeasure or indignation at some act, remark, person, etc. As a leading lady, we have many opportunities to become resentful. Our position is not an easy position but it's imperative that we guard our hearts from being offended and resentful. In Luke 6:35 in the Amplified, it says the Father is kind and charitable and good to the ungrateful and the selfish and wicked. We definitely have some ungrateful, selfish and even wicked people in our ministries but we are required to love them no matter what. Jesus goes on to say to be merciful (sympathetic, tender, responsive, and compassionate) even as your Father is [all these.] That has been my prayer to be more compassionate to the ungrateful, selfish and even wicked. I could go on and on with what the Lord showed me in the scriptures He gave me. I was actually going to do a video to preach it! Just be aware about what comes out of your mouth when certain names are mentioned. Are you speaking positive or negative? Are you staying quiet and prayerful?

Love is not "touchy or fretful or resentful; it takes no account of the evil done to it." I Cor. 13:5 AMP

Leading Ladies are not resentful.

Ladder Holders

You know we go through seasons in ministry. Seasons of growth, transition, assessment. It's so important to stop and assess your position. If we don't take time to look at the hard things, we don't change. Recently, we had one of those times when you just couldn't put your finger on it but there was just a heaviness that had come upon many in the church, including myself. Don't get me wrong we were still moving forward, worshipping, the presence of God flowing but there was something that just wasn't quite right. Unknowingly, I had let a burden or weight just come upon me. Then my husband shared that he had felt this weight. We had other leaders say they felt it too. Again, there wasn't ONE situation that we could say it was. Two weeks ago, I was teaching a Life Group and showed a video on the subject of having good Ladder Holders. (I highly recommend you getting that teaching by

Samuel Chan. It will really help your leaders and yourself.) Every leader needs to have someone holding their ladder. The higher you go, the bigger ladder you need and the more ladder holders you will require. I felt like we just didn't have the ladder holders. Like no one else had the passion and focus to help us carry the vision. You see when you become weighted down you feel like you have it all on your shoulders and no one sees you're carrying it all standing on the ladder at the same time. You feel like no one cares that you're about to fall off this ladder. I share with you and others that it's not for us to carry but somehow I can easily take on the responsibility of it all. What about you?

Let me tell you what happened the same day that I taught that Life Group. That night after a meeting and before the evening service, I went into the office and all our pastors and our elders were in the office standing around the walls. They began to tell us how they were in this with my husband and I. That they were holding our ladders. They began to wash our feet! Ladies, a huge weight fell off of me that night! My husband cried, I mean, cried! This made me really lose it because then I knew he was going through what I was going through. That night I shouted, "NO MORE will I shoulder the load!" I think it really sunk in that I have ladder holders.

I know that heaviness was meant to stop us because it even was affecting the atmosphere in our home and in our communications towards one another. It was broken in Jesus name! In Psalm 81:6 the Father tells us that He removes my shoulder from the burden. His yoke is easy and His burden is light. (Matthew 11:30) That night my precious pastors and elders helped me to cast my burden on the Lord. (Psalm 55:22) We can't do ministry alone.

I'm praying for each of you to have people come around you and hold your arms up. I'm holding your arms up, my dear sister! You are more than a conqueror and nothing is going to take you out! God didn't call you and your husband to fail but to SUCCEED! In the hard times, I remind the Lord that He was the one who called us and I know He didn't call us here to fail. So I just want to encourage you to not take on the load. When you realize you have taken it all on your shoulders, roll it off quickly. Pray for some good ladder holders and if you have some, tell them you need help. I'm thankful our ladder holders were looking out for us.

Bridle the Tongue & Bless Your Husband

I have a huge praise report that I just have to share! My husband and I went on a trip to North Carolina to celebrate our pastors (the pastor we were saved under) 75th birthday. We are slightly crazy because we drove 10 hours right through a tropical storm. When we were pulling up to the hotel, my husband said, "That was the best trip that I think we have ever had! I enjoyed being with you!" I was jumping up and down on the inside! You see, most of the time, I tend to say the wrong thing and get all up in my feelings or talk incessantly about church and the issues that come with it. When I do these things, it frustrates my husband because he just wants to check out sometimes. This trip was different because I just let him talk and if he asked for my thoughts or opinion, he was better able to receive it. Needless to say, I just relaxed.

I've been meditating on this verse, "If anyone thinks himself to be religious (piously observant of the external duties of his faith) and does not bridle his tongue but deludes his own heart, this person's religious service is worthless (futile, barren)." (James 1:26 AMP) I believe that the only way to change is through the Word. The scripture says to "bridle" the tongue which means to control, hold back, or restrain. I want everything that I do to be fruitful, not fruitless and worthless. So, I don't have to say everything I think about every situation. Maybe you've got a hold on this quickly, but this has been a struggle for me that I'm overcoming. My desire is to be "perfect (growing into complete maturity of godliness in mind and character, having reached the proper height of virtue and integrity)," as my heavenly Father is perfect (Matt. 5:48 AMP). I'm slowly getting that ministry isn't mine to shoulder. People will be people. I just had to share my small but BIG victory with you! Leading Ladies are focused to kill those small foxes that can be destructive if left unchecked!

I pray that my thoughts and revelations have been a blessing to you. Hopefully you have been encouraged to know that you are not alone! We are in this together. I challenge you to reach out and to other pastors' wives. There are many who are crying out for friendships. I pray that you will be a confident Leading Lady that supports your husband in his calling. Most of all, my prayer is that you will be an example to the many women who are watching you. May you enjoy the journey and live healthy and full of joy!

Made in the USA
Middletown, DE
27 July 2024

58042750R00080